Understanding Everyday Experience

Series Editor: Laurie Taylor

For Catherine and Peter
who never make me feel old

MARY STOTT

Ageing for Beginners

BASIL BLACKWELL · OXFORD

© Mary Stott 1981

First published in 1981 by
Basil Blackwell Publisher Ltd
108 Cowley Road
Oxford OX4 1JF
England

British Library Cataloguing in Publication Data

Stott, Mary
    Ageing for beginners. — (Understanding
    everyday experience).
    1. Old age
    I. Title   II. Series
    301.43'5   HQ1061

ISBN 0-631-11591-9
ISBN 0-631-12777-1 Pbk

Typesetting by Cambrian Typesetters
Farnborough, Hants
Printed in Great Britain at the
Alden Press, Oxford

Contents

Preface

I just about admit to my age of forty-four. Only once or twice, and then while far from home, have I knocked a year or two off or pretended that I am other than solidly middle-aged. But I have always been reluctant to consider the meaning of growing older. Somehow it seemed enough to admit publicly that the years were passing without also dwelling on the consequences of their passage. Like many other people I was frightened to stare hard at the future: it reminded me far too forcibly of the fact of my own mortality.

This book has dispelled much of the fear and anxiety I formally felt. It is essential reading for anyone who has tried, like myself, to duck questions about their own ageing: what they will look like, where they will live, what others will think of them, what will amuse or comfort them. It is not about old age or the biological processes of ageing, but about the immense variety of experience and activity which awaits everyone in future years. It is, in other words, thoroughly critical of the 'ageism' in our society, the belief that it is reasonable to talk of people principally in terms of a chronological category, rather than on the basis of their needs, desires and capabilities.

It is not surprising that Mary Stott has written such

a brave, humane and moving book. As a successful feature writer on the *Guardian,* she has for a period of more than twenty years listened with patience and good humour to readers who recognize from her columns that she is someone who will understand and appreciate what they are saying. She is also someone who has tried in her writing to cope with her own biographical dilemmas. In fact, it was her sensitive essay on life after the death of her husband which initially led us to invite her to contribute to this new series, *Understanding Everyday Experience.*

The aim of the series is straightforward. It seeks to show that a whole range of experiences — sexual anxieties, feelings of loneliness and loss, of physical disability or incompetence, of growing up, coping with middle age and ageing — are at some time or another, and with varying degrees of intensity, aspects of all our lives. That is, they are not necessarily 'problems', matters for medication or treatment, or for treatises or textbooks by doctors and psychiatrists. The books in the series will set out, therefore, to 'reclaim' some of these experiences from the specialists and return them to the everyday world, and in that way demonstrate that they are far more manageable than they might otherwise have seemed. Fortunately, there is no need for any detailed account of how this will be achieved. The following pages provide the best possible illustration.

Laurie Taylor

1
Images

Shakespeare died when he was fifty-three. So what did he know about growing old? When he put into Jaques's mouth the image of the 'slipper'd pantaloon', with his 'shrunk shank' and 'big manly voice, turning again towards childish treble', he was about thirty-five — just the age when people have a sudden panic fear that now they are poised on the crest of a downward slope. Millions of us since *As You Like It* was first staged have proved Jaques a false prophet about the 'seventh age' of man:

> Second childishness, and mere oblivion,
> Sans teeth, sans eyes, sans taste, sans everything.

and it is because I have no conscious fear of this decrepitude, as I enter my eighth decade, that I write this book. It is not just to share thoughts and experiences with my contemporaries; not even just to hearten men and women on the point of retirement. It is also to try to convince the middle-aged that they are frightening themselves unnecessarily and creating false images of ageing which do no good to any of us.

A character in Kate Millett's *Sita* reflects: 'If I was forty I was on longer young; when you are no longer young you are old. Old age is only the tedious and

1

debilitating prelude to death, being dead while still minimally alive.' It is seldom the elderly who go on and on about the awfulness of being old. Maggie Kuhn, leader of the American Grey Panthers, said that old age should be a 'flowering'. George Bernard Shaw decided at sixty that he had got his 'seventh wind' and, according to his biographer, attained a delightful sense of freedom and became 'adventurous and irresponsible'. The spectres which could so easily haunt us are projections of the fears of younger people of the loss of the powers that are so important to them. It is a fact that only a very small percentage of us are going to end up blind and boring or deaf and daft, and it is salutary to remember that a small percentage of us might also have been gravely injured in a car crash in our twenties, or smitten with polio or multiple sclerosis in our thirties. All the ills that flesh is heir to do not wait to descend on us in our seventh or eighth decade, and what the young see when they look at us is by no means always what we know about ourselves.

In her diaries Virginia Woolf left a sharply etched portrait of her friend Margaret Llewelyn Davies and her companion and assistant Lilian Harris, who for over thirty years had devoted their lives to building up the Women's Co-operative Guild: 'They sit beside the corpse of the Women's Guild; the blinds are drawn; they are sad and white, brave, tearless but infinitely mournful. I see what happens. When one leaves one's life work at 60 one dies. Death, at least, must be seen to be there, visible, expectant.' Of Lilian Harris she says two even more bitter things: 'Then Lilian Harris with her hands on her lap, facing old age and horribly bored', and 'We dragged Lilian over to Richmond but she saw nothing but the ground. Very unhappy, she said she was.' But ten years or so later I saw Miss Davies and Miss Harris in their serene and pleasant home in Surrey and had no such picture of boredom and misery. They kept in touch, and many hundreds of working-class women to whom they had given confidence and vision knew their worth. (It was, in fact, poor Virginia who could not bear the burden of life.)

Women writers of today, even the most perceptive and sympathetic of them, still tend to see us as spectres of what they fear to become — as, for example, Jill Tweedie in the *Guardian*:

Do so many men have to grow pear-shaped bellies? Do so many old women have to wear frizzy white perms and cover their bodies in shapeless clothes, summer or winter, poor or rich? . . . Whenever I pass a group of old men or old women I can hear the keening note in their voices as they list for each other the iniquities of today . . .. The elderly are remarkably conformist, no matter how unique each of them might have been in their youth, which is why younger people have difficulty in regarding them as individuals . . .. Old age has a vested interest in decline, a profit motive in refusing to acknowledge improvement . . ..

Sometimes one is made painfully aware that in our Western youth-oriented culture old age has become a terrible disease, as shameful as head lice in children and VD in their older siblings. Ivor Brown, critic, editor and author, called this 'one of the idiocies of our time' in his splendid book on ageing, *Old and Young,* published when he was eighty. He spotted the description 'gerontophobia' as early as 1968, in the

3

Spectator. Maggie Kuhn thinks there is a serious epidemic of 'gerontophobia' in the United States today. And of course it afflicts not only the young but the elderly as well. 'There is a lot of self-hate in "gerontophobia",' she said on British TV. 'You hate your hands, you hate your wrinkles, you hate your grey hairs.' And because we are ashamed of our age and condition we lie about it, dye our hair or have transplants and face lifts. We censor our conversational references to political and other events, however interesting and relevant, that happened before the Second World War, for they would reveal that we were adult nearly half a century ago.

We are apt to forget the extent to which the communications industry is in the hands of the young and the young middle-aged. It is their images of ageing that need to be rethought. A schoolboy interviewed by Ronald Blythe for his fine book *The View in Winter* said, 'When you read about old people in the papers or see programmes about them on television, they are always shown as sad and ill and lonely.' Programme-makers, novelists, playwrights, journalists in all media want above all nowadays to be 'realistic' — which seems to mean seeing situations always in black and grey. Painters use shadow to define shape, not to obscure it. Writers might remember that.

It isn't so much dislike of the old that undermines our confidence, though that does exist, but patronage and pity. Even the best intentioned people assume that they, like Nanny, know best what is good for us. I was taken aback to see a whole-page advertisement, inserted by the Health Education Council in the *Guardian* of all newspapers, about the danger of dying from hypothermia: 'The old can die from the cold without even noticing it.' The text went like this,

4

imaginatively set out so that we should be quite sure to get the message:

When you are old you can become cold without even noticing it.

Often without a shiver.

You simply slow down.

The next thing you don't notice is your

mind slowing down. Did you order the

meal? You can't remember. Never mind.

Now you've really slowed down.

You feel drowsy. Even the effort

of going to bed seems too much.

You just nod off in the chair.

It doesn't seem to matter very

much.

I should have thought it would have been clear, even to the youngest advertising executive, that people mentally alert enough to read the *Guardian* daily are not the sort of people who need lessons on hypo-thermia. But the image-makers envisage protecting the elderly against themselves or against the hazards of life, and this sort of image is in common use. Perhaps it is unconscious revenge on those who 'nan-nied' them in their childhood — as in the story of the two women whom Dr Alex Comfort, the gerontologist, watched in a cinema. One, an elderly woman, was trying to adjust her watch. Her daughter snatched it, and the mother said, 'Why don't you ever let me wind my watch? I haven't wound it yet and I've had it a year.'

The daughter said, 'But you're turning the hands the wrong way.'

'I'm not trying to wind it, dear,' said the mother. 'I'm setting the time.'

The imagined pathos of old age is exploited quite deliberately in, for example, the fund-raising advertisements of Help the Aged. It is a technique that has been used in the past to unloose purse-strings by Dr Barnardo's and the National Society for the Prevention of Cruelty to Children and, more recently, by Shelter. But I would not serve as a model for such photographs for a million pounds — because I am not to be pitied. Nor are millions of the laughably designated 'senior citizens' whose assumed needs have to be caricatured to persuade people to part with their cash. Even some of the authors and production editors of useful and informative books on retirement and ageing need a sharp new look at the images they project — on the book jackets, for instance. Photographs show jolly old men kissing jolly old women or standing cosily shoulder to shoulder . . . but the old men are likely to be toothless and wearing cloth caps, and the old women are generally photographed in profile, emphasizing their sagging jaws and scrawny necks. Is this preference for the faintly comic working-class image subconsciously self-protective? We, who do not wear cloth caps, will never be like that; it is The Others who will lose their hair and their teeth and develop pot-bellies and dropped bosoms.

Why don't they — and we — take our images from those splendid, sharp-witted and positively inspiring peers of the realm, the Lords Shinwell, Fenner

Brockway and Noel-Baker, and the Lady Wootton of Abinger (the first woman to take her seat on the Woolsack)? There are many men and women in their eighties and even nineties whom it would be an unthinkable impertinence to deride with the sort of instant snapshot that can make even men and women of forty look repulsive.

Why do there have to be *any* images of 'old age'? There used, I suppose, to be images of 'middle age' — 'fair, fat and forty' — but that kind of thing has passed out of fashion since women became more independent and developed more obviously individual personalities. If we do not typecast nineteen-year-olds, there is certainly no reason to typecast ninety-year-olds. They are, in fact, likely to have acquired with the years more emphatic, sharply defined characters. And whether this is so or not, we know that people remain themselves, however long they live, and never become carbon copies of one another, with the same needs, wishes, skills, prejudices, likings. Any one of us in our seventh, eighth and even ninth decade, looking in the mirror, sees himself, herself, as not essentially different from the young person of fifty years ago. When the grandchildren look through the snapshot albums and say, 'Was that you, Granny? Did you really look like that, Grandpa?' you are surprised, for to yourself you have not altered much. The wrapping may have got somewhat discoloured and tatty with long use, but the content is not greatly changed. On a Brains Trust panel, the scientist Dr Bronowski, a notable communicator, said that it felt exactly the same being old: 'I look on the world with exactly the same eyes.'

So we do, even if those eyes need stronger glasses and if our ears tell us that most people mumble nowadays. We are *people*, not a Problem, not a category, not a separate species. To quote Ronald Blythe again:

> One of the fearful developments in the consciousness of many old people is that, in the eyes of society, they have become another species. Ironically, an intensive caring and concern for their welfare is frequently more likely to suggest this relegation than indifference and neglect. The growing bureaucracy, amateur and professional, voluntary and state, for dealing with geriatrics makes some old folk feel they no longer quite belong to the human race any more. They want those who really know them as human beings to speak for them. To tell these efficient planners who appear to be coralling them off from other generations who they really are.

Conferences I have been to where social workers, paid and unpaid, come together from all over the United Kingdom to listen to professors and politicians orating on how to deal with the 'recreationally inert', or with the 'creeping emergency' of the growth in the numbers of very old people, or with 'social gerontology', or with the 'psychodynamics of human relations' are less apt to depress me than to make me angry. Do these excellent people, categorizing the elderly, isolating them as a problem in our society, not realize that they are us and we are them? Do their imaginations switch off at the point of realization that they too, day by day, are becoming old, and that they too may one day be talked about and discussed as if they were some threatened — or threatening — animal species? Don't they see that some of us want to retort, 'How would *you* like it, chum?'?

Anyone feeling uneasy about the approach of retirement and old age should hasten to read Alex Comfort's invigorating book *A Good Age,* as funny as it is subversive of accepted attitudes. One quotation must suffice:

> Never let 'old' go past when it's used as a put-down. You could be good-natured and say that there's many a good tune played on an old fiddle, or that you're no older than they, you've only been around longer; but squelch the implication. This is a part of the shaping of society — behavioural psychology teaches that if you alter people's verbal behaviour, you alter them.

Images of old age as a condition are mostly a menace. They should be exorcised, like evil spirits. But that is no reason why human beings of any age should not have their personal pin-ups, their admired models, their inspiration. It isn't any use aspiring to Beatrice and Sidney Webb's analytical thinking, right into their great old age, but one can emulate the spirit of their partnership: 'What does it matter what two "Over Seventies" think, say or do, so long as they do not whine about getting old and go merrily along, hand in hand, to the end of the road?' One can bask in the thought that age has added wisdom and dignity to Harold Macmillan's political view, or an acid incisiveness to Dame Rebecca West's critical reviews. Should we not gather a handful of adjectives and try them for fit, like hats or shoes? 'Indomitable', like Artur Rubinstein, giving a Carnegie Hall piano recital at the age of eighty-nine, when he could not even see the keys, let alone the printed music? 'Eccentric', like Edith Sitwell, with her splendid Tudor jewellery and clothes? 'Steadfast', like Lord Noel-Baker, still lecturing powerfully and succinctly on world peace at the age of ninety-plus? J. B. Priestley cheerfully accepts 'grumpy'; Ivor Brown rather liked to think of himself as an 'old buffer'.

Many of us have twenty years after retirement in which to earn an epitaph. I envy the people, great or humble, whom their friends will remember as forthright and fearless, but I think the tribute I would like best to have deserved is that paid by Ivor Brown to Professor Gilbert Murray: 'There was a radiance of gentle wisdom from the chair in which he sat, with a foot muff under him.'

There's no law against dreaming, is there? No law against imagining, with W. B. Yeats, a land

> Where nobody gets old and godly and grave
> Where nobody gets old and crafty and wise
> Where nobody gets old and bitter of tongue.

But I sometimes wish there were a law against 'ageism', and some way of preventing people from substituting for our pleasant dreams of serene detachment nightmares of loneliness, poverty and mindless decrepitude. It wasn't like that, was it, for your mother and father, for all your uncles and aunts, your godparents and your second cousins once removed? Why should the prospect of ageing be a nightmare for *you*?

2
Places

People need places . . . places to be at home. Once, many years ago, an Englishwoman said to a little girl, a 'displaced person' in a refugee camp, 'We shall be able to find a home for you and your family soon.' 'Oh,' said the child, 'we've got a home. All we need is a house to put it in.'

Most people coming up to retirement age have a home. What begins to bother them is whether the home is in the right place — the right house, the right neighbourhood, the right town, even the right country. There is nothing odd about this. Most people move house two or three times in their adult life — from the first bed-sit or shared flat to the first small marital home; then to a semi-detached or refurbished terraced house as the family increases; then, if they are lucky, to a more substantial house, often in the outer suburbs, as the children become teenagers, and then again when the family shrinks. It is an excellent thing that the structure in which the family 'home' is housed should expand or contract according to the needs of its owners.

So many people have written so many awful warnings about moving house after retirement that it hardly seems necessary to repeat them. Don't move to a place where you don't know anyone; don't move to the top of a hill or the top of a house; don't move

11

more than ten minutes' walk from the shops, the station, the bus stop or the church, library or club. Don't forget that you will in time become less mobile; don't forget that if you move far away you will have to build up a new network of services as well as of friends and occupations — a new doctor and dentist, a new plumber, electrician, builder, laundry. It will probably be necessary to get to know a new tax inspector and bank manager, possibly a new accountant and solicitor, and it is not very easy to sort out the people who will suit your needs if you have no reliable personal acquaintances in the area.

But don't think that if you *do* move, it is an irrevocable step. If your new home doesn't fit as comfortably as well-worn shoes, you don't have to stay there. You should have the courage to make another move as soon as you find what seems right for you — having learned by experience what *isn't* right. Don't wait too long. One grows more liable to give way to apathy and inertia as one grows older. My own story is quite a good object lesson about house-moving, especially, but not only, for widows or widowers. Having come to the conclusion, slowly but positively, that the house in which I had lived very happily for twenty years with my husband was far too big for one person, I set about flat-hunting in London, to be nearer to my daughter, my only child. We scoured the neighbourhood for quite some time and at last found a three-roomed flat at the top of a house in a mid-Victorian terrace. I was able to 'improve' it with fitted wardrobes and kitchen cupboards and moved with as much of my furniture and possessions as I could fit in. I rather enjoyed drawing plans and diagrams of what was to go where, and most of them worked out all right.

I was quite reasonably happy in this new nest, but

various drawbacks gradually became evident. It was on a main road and the traffic noise at night was bothersome. The stairs were not much of a trial — they might be now, ten years later — but the hall and stairs' linoleum had to be polished by each resident in turn, one week in three. One could only reach the dustbins by walking down two flights of stairs, along a passage under the side of the house and right to the bottom of the garden. I seldom put the washing out, though this was permitted at certain times; I seldom sat in the garden and did a minimum of gardening, because none of the garden ever seemed to belong to me. But what increasingly bothered me was being so cut off from the actual earth. It may sound an absurd fancy, but perhaps it could have turned into a real deprivation. Twenty years or so of being able to walk straight out into the garden and pull a few seeding weeds or cut off a few dead roses had become part of the pattern of my life.

This feeling that one needs to be near the earth is not as eccentric as I thought it might be. I met a retired single woman on the seventh floor of a large housing trust block of flats who used exactly the words I had used to myself. 'I miss being near the earth' — and the flat in which she had lived for forty years had actually been a semi-basement, giving her a view only of pavements and feet walking by. On her seventh floor she had splendid views of waving trees and the grassy slopes of a neighbouring park, which would have been exhilarating to many a town-dweller. Many people, I know, feel oppressed by 'all those people on top of me', on the ground floor or in the basement of a large house or block. But for this woman there was the need to be 'near the earth.' One can only say, 'Know thyself.'

One happy day my daughter showed me a flat in a house very near to her own. Even looking through the windows and down the long, neglected walled garden, I felt a tug. This was the sort of place my 'home' needed. It is called on documents the 'basement flat' and by estate agents, more temptingly, the 'garden flat'. What lifts my heart is that level with my bedroom windows there is the green, green grass, a forsythia, a large old fuchsia, a birdtable and whatever flowers I have planted. Front and back there are great cedars where pigeons and crows roost and where squirrels sometimes race up and down. Mirrors on almost every wall bring the sky and the trees and ivy-covered walls right into my dwelling. My home and I settled down in this flat like a dog into its basket. Here we are, and here we hope to stay, in a quiet little road, between a junior high school for girls, and a morning playgroup for toddlers.

Not everyone needs or wants to move before or just after retirement. Not everyone *can* move easily. It is estimated that only about half of all pensioner households are owner-occupied dwellings. The remaining pensioners are in rented accommodation, more than two-thirds of which is provided by public authorities. And we should not forget that over a quarter of households headed by people over sixty-five are in homes which lack at least one basic amenity, bath, hot water or inside w.c. Those who are owner-occupiers have only to find a purchaser for their outgrown house or flat and a seller of accommodation better fitted to their present needs. The others who pay rent either to a private landlord or to a local authority or, more rarely, to a housing trust or co-operative are virtually dependent on being able to arrange an exchange, which means going on a local authority or housing association list. Until the national stock of dwellings is nearer to meeting the demand, there will be virtually no unfurnished accommodation advertised for rent. You cannot give up your tenancy, however burdensome the rent or the household chores, until you have somewhere to go. For most people hope must rest with the local authorities, with their immense queues of applicants and shortage of suitable 'lets' for retired people. No wonder most people stay on in their own homes, even if it becomes a struggle.

The housing needs of a normal couple in their early sixties are very similar to the needs of a newly married pair. They are no more looking for 'special' accommodation than are the newlyweds, but any points system is bound to rate the newlyweds higher than the retired couple, because of the expectation of children. If the retired couple are allocated a flat or bungalow, it is almost bound to be in a development built for the elderly-to-aged, though this is probably not what most of us would choose. We are accustomed to living in a mixed-age community, and that is what seems natural and right.

However, to get things into perspective one must take a quick look back at what retirement from the work force meant in terms of places to live for our grandparents and great-grandparents. We should remember the time when people who could no longer earn a weekly wage and pay their rent had only two possibilities — living with sons and daughters or going into the workhouse. It is, after all, less than a hundred years since there was any pension at all for the aged, and I am certain that fear of the workhouse dominated the thinking of many older people right up to the Second World War, even those who had good supportive sons and daughters. The image was so vivid, the possibility so horrifying, for those who, through unemployment, ill-health or ill-fortune, had not been able to save enough to exist on. Even in the inflation-free twenties, the number of wage earners who could contribute enough to insurance schemes to secure a realistic income from the age of sixty-five upwards must have been very small.

The fear of destitution goes back a very long way — certainly as far back as the dissolution of the monasteries, which swept away most provision for the sick and the old and left them dependent on the 'parish'. It was the Poor Relief Act of 1601 which set up the first 'Poorhouses' and kept the old and ill alive. It wasn't until 1834 that Parliament took a hand in regulating the provision of care for those unable to care for themselves. It was grudging care, though. A basic principle was laid down, which lingers on today, that those given relief should not be allowed conditions as good as, let alone better than, those of the 'independent labourer of the lowest class'.

Despite the fact that the Industrial Revolution had totally changed the lives and possibilities of working men and women, despite the fact that the population was growing rapidly and too many families had too many mouths to feed, the idea persisted that poverty was due to laziness, irresponsibility or dissolute habits. This idea also lingers on today in the minds of some middle-class people, especially those who have risen in the social scale by their own efforts and fail to understand why every other able-bodied citizen cannot do likewise.

Building workhouses for paupers was undoubtedly a laudable intention and a big step forward in its day. The Victorians were full of energy as well as organizational skill. They set about dividing the country up

16

into more than 600 'unions' (an old name for the workhouse) and launched a programme of workhouse building which makes our own housing programme look meagre. Hundreds of workhouses were built in the 1830s and 1840s. They must have gratified the philanthropic outlook of many good Christians. Were they originally welcomed by the poor men and women who might otherwise have been left to die in their hovels or even in the streets? We don't know. We do know that to end one's days in a workhouse was soon to become the most dreaded fate, both shameful and painful. And to us this is no wonder — by 1839 the average workhouse catered for about 400 paupers. We have all seen those grim buildings; many are still in use, refurbished as hospitals, but still bleak from outside.

The deterrent aspect of the Poor Law was generally regarded as of the utmost importance. It was an Awful Warning to the children of the Aged Poor and others to make sure that they were worthy of a better fate. It was as it were a penalty, even a just punishment, for the improvident as well as for the dissolute. It is painful now to realize that even that courageous and far-sighted Fabian, Beatrice Webb, in her Minority Report on the Poor Law in 1909, took the view that the number of the 'undeserving poor' was 'so large as to be a problem to be dealt with rigorously'. There was, she wrote, 'no inconsiderable number of old men and women whose persistent addiction to drink makes it necessary to refuse them any but institutional provision'. She thought that the 'destitution authority' made 'not a bad provision', and she reckoned that a workhouse, with its dull routine and deterrent regulations, was probably a fitting place to end a misspent life.

The seed of the Welfare State had germinated though. The first old age pension was introduced in 1911 by David Lloyd George — for many years some people called their 5-shilling pittance 'my Lloyd George'. It was not nearly enough to live on even then, but it was just enough to make a retired father or a widowed mother a bit more welcome in their children's homes and so keep them out of the workhouse. The workhouses were still there though, and were not seriously questioned by any but a few socialists as a proper provision for those who had no other income and no family able and willing to take them in. When the first majority Labour Government was returned in 1945 a new look soon became evident. A Nuffield Foundation Survey set up in 1944 reported very strongly in 1947 that small houses, of thirty to thirty-five beds, should be substituted for workhouse provision for the elderly and suggested that several thousand would be needed in the next fifteen to twenty years. In 1947, introducing the National Assistance Bill, Aneurin Bevan declared, 'The workhouse is to go. Although people have tried to humanize it, it was in many respects an evil institution.'

It was widely believed, and often stated categorically, that the workhouse was doomed. So it was, in the long term, but a very thorough and detailed study of institutions and homes for the aged, initiated by Peter Townsend in the later fifties, revealed that workhouses were still in use. In his illuminating and often shocking book *The Last Refuge* Peter Townsend declared, 'In 1960 workhouses were still the mainstay of local authority residential services for the handicapped and aged, and accounted for just over half the accommodation used by county and county borough councils, for just over half the residents and probably over three-fifths of the old people actually admitted to community care in the course of a year.' There were then over 300 such institutions and many contained more than 250 beds.

Of course, by the fifties the deterrent aspect of the workhouse had been obliterated — but it was still a place of dread. A reason for this that one finds quite shocking now is that the segregation of the sexes was taken almost as a matter of course, even though this meant separating husbands and wives. There were not very many married couples in institutions at the time of Peter Townsend's survey, but there certainly were some, and they were normally living in separate wards or even in different blocks. One can see how convenient this arrangement might be for staff — far fewer problems with bathroom and toilet facilities and with nursing those confined to bed. But the cruelty of sundering husbands and wives who had lived in amity and affectionate mutual support for forty or fifty years hardly bears thinking about.

One of the saddest stories in Peter Townsend's book is an interview with a wife who said, 'They said we could be together when we came here, and that we'd only be parted at night, but it isn't so. They don't want him in the ladies' rooms and they say, "No gentlemen allowed in here" when he comes along . . . we can't be together. We're separated.' I would have said that that couldn't happen today, but at the national Pensioners' Convention organized by the Trades Union Congress in June 1979 a delegate from the Kent and Sussex Federation of Old Age Pensioners told of a couple married for fifty-three years who were in different homes in different villages and could see one another perhaps once a month.

It is true that a great many women, not all of them

19

elderly, object vigorously to being treated in mixed wards, and object still more to being washed or given the bedpan by a man or *in the hearing* of male patients. Probably the men mind mixed wards less than women — and certainly accept the intimate physical care of women nurses — because nursing has always been acceptable as carry-over from the care of one's mother. Moreover, the resistance by women to the presence of men around the day wards is in part an aspect of an old female joke — the equivalent of the male joke about being henpecked. Also, there are women who have always found marriage more of a misery than a pleasure and who are quite glad to be on their own at last, free of the demands of an intolerant and intolerable old man. But such marriages are few, and the need for 'married quarters' should be given priority in every housing scheme, even though it is perfectly well-known that elderly women outnumber elderly men by at least three to one.

The greater capacity for survival among women does make for certain severe practical difficulties in allocating protected accommodation. In a home for the very old and incapacitated in Manchester I found the management committee had had to close its doors to men because they were such a tiny minority among the applicants that to admit one man almost inevitably meant that three places in the normal four-bedded room would have to remain unused. There is such a need for this kind of 'last-refuge' accommodation that such a waste of beds could not be allowed. But where do the displaced old men go?

Age Concern has estimated that more than 2,000,000 elderly people live alone. This is the sort of statistic that is used to wring hearts and to open purses. But though living alone may be wretched and frightening, it can also be very pleasant for those who have good health, many interests and suitable accommodation – once they have made the painful adjustment to the loss of a lifetime partner. It is right that local authorities should build more and more accommodation for elderly people, because there are going to be very many more elderly and truly aged people at the end of the century. But most people are not *ready* to go into special accommodation the moment they retire or, indeed, for quite a number of years afterwards. If they do put their names on elderly housing lists, it is often because it seems the only way to safeguard their future. Perhaps they live in rented accommodation owned by a landlord who wants to get them out so that he can redevelop the property and let it for very high rents. One local Age Concern group told me that one of their housing advisers' most important functions is to help pensioners who are subject to harassment by landlords. Or again, a retired couple may have an excellent house which is obviously too big for them to maintain comfortably. The wife may be a bit too stiff in the knees to keep six rooms clean and tidy; the husband may be a bit short of wind for mowing a largish lawn and digging the vegetable patch; or the rates and cost of fuel may become a serious burden.

What such people may want is a grant to divide their home into two more or less self-contained units. Local authority housing departments should investigate these possibilities much more energetically. Many people, perhaps most, *like* living where they are accustomed to live; most can live there safely, as well as happily, right into old age if good neighbours or street wardens keep a watchful eye on them and see that the available services are provided when needed.

But house conversion has its drawbacks. Many elderly people have a deep-seated fear of being unable to get rid of a tenant who has become disagreeable to them. Tenants', as well as owners', rights have to be respected, for they also need a home, but all humans, like most animals, tend to be possessive of their territory. Perhaps as we grow older we tend to become still more resentful of any encroachment on it. In this situation a tenant can be regarded, obsessively, as an enemy invader.

Most of us are going to be hale and hearty throughout our sixties and seventies, and many of us will be perfectly happy in our own homes well into our eighties, but it is only common sense to have contingency plans at the back of our minds, and to give a sharp, even if brief, look at the pros and cons. Supposing we stay on where we are. Even if the house or flat is not too big or too far from the shops and bus stop, we may at some distant date become more or less housebound. Is the community going to be able to prop us up and provide for all our needs — home helps, meals on wheels, district nurse and so on? And ought we to *expect* all this as a right? The experienced and very sympathetic principal executive officer of the National Federation of Housing Associations put it like this to me:

> We must respect the right of the individual to stay put. But it seems to me there has to come a point where if a person says, 'I am going to stay here until I die' and the only way to achieve this is by a massive injection of home helps, district nurses and so on for ten years or more, the community's resources have got to be assessed against the alternatives. Is it going to be better all round to give

these elderly persons a chance to move somewhere else which will give them a chance to look after themselves a bit better and with less 'input' by society?

So what are the possibilities if we make up our minds to move? For a fortunate few there is the possibility of a total change of life — moving to a warmer climate, pulling up our roots, and settling in the south of France, Spain, Portugal, Italy, a Greek island or wherever a series of happy holidays has suggested that life would be paradisal. The dream is fulfilled for some, but not by any means for all. The people who retired to Malta and settled there before the island severed its last ties with Britain almost all wanted to stay on among its friendly people and in its delightful climate. The people who invested in charming villas in Cyprus found that civil war between the Greek and Turkish Cypriots destroyed their future and left them with mortgages to pay off on looted, damaged and un-lettable property. People who enjoy visits to their holiday homes in the Dordogne may find that living there month after month is less enchanting. Friends who retired to the Algarve told me:

We think it is advisable to rent a place in the country of your choice for at least a year before taking the final plunge. Climates are never what the publicists make out. Winters are often very disagreeable, with heavy rainfall instead of frost and snow, and perhaps the cold is less trying than the intense humidity of a country like Portugal.

People who, like me, have spent a January holiday

in a climate like Malta's will know also that Mediterranean homes are seldom equipped to soften chilly
winters. The floors are tiled; there is no central heating and no double-glazing. In a flat in St Paul's Bay,
Malta, I was so cold in January that for days at a time
I wore two vests, two pairs of knickers, two pairs of
trousers, two jerseys and two jackets . . . and on one
beastly cold night sat huddled by a tiny electric fire
with a hot water bottle on my knees! Obviously, if
one were living in a Mediterranean resort permanently,
one would see that there were various forms of heating
for the short, sharp winter, but people who only visit
the Mediterranean in the lovely spring, summer and
autumn months should certainly spend a winter there
before making a final decision about a move.

> People usually choose a region with an existing
> English-speaking community [my friends went on
> to say]. There is usually quite a flourishing social
> life. This may or may not quickly become boring,
> according to the individual's personality. If you
> like golf (and can afford it), and if you can enjoy
> bridge and like going to cocktail parties and enjoy
> meeting the same people all the time, you may
> settle well. It really all depends on what your life-
> style was in your country of origin. Generally
> speaking, cultural activities are non-existent.

[That certainly would not apply to Malta, where
British and Maltese enjoy many cultural pursuits
together, especially music and amateur dramatics.]

> There is not the compensation, we find, of good
> television. Most of the community will be retired
> people, which can be depressing, with everyone

looking back on their past experiences and achievements.

It is lack of any stimulus that makes the days drag. The happiest among us are the people who have retired from posts in the old Colonies or have worked most of their lives abroad in similar closed societies. Another drawback of life in a Mediterranean 'haven' is that there is, of course, a summer invasion of visitors. Having new faces around can give one a fillip, but it is not all joy for the residents. Some are against the visitors on principle ('These damn tourists!'), and for all of us shopping can become a great bore, with long queues and soaring prices in shops and bars.

In the nine years we have lived here there have been no births, a great many of us have died, many have gone back home and there are very, very few of the 'originals' left. Now we can see that the dream was just a dream.

There is, of course, the bonus of escaping British income tax, but one must offset against this the fact that there are usually no health services abroad in any way comparable to our much-maligned English ones. In fact [wrote my friends] one had really better not be really ill out here. We are fortunate in having a very competent English-speaking Portuguese doctor, but he has just left on a month's holiday, and he has never heard of the 'locum' system which we take for granted.

Troubled by this rather sad account of life in a lovely climate, I got in touch with another friend who now also lives with her husband in Portugal — not in an English-speaking colony, but in an inland village where, she says:

25

to be constantly out of doors is heaven, without mufflers, coats, socks, wellies and gloves. Also the birds are a joy. We had a pair of swallows nesting just where we breakfast and saw them hatch, feed and finally fly five youngsters. There are hoopoos on the lawn and partridges, and occasionally the flash of a golden oriel. I suppose many people would be bored stiff. Not enough life. No shops. Still, we have saints' days and fiestas when it is possible to dance through the night, drink wine and eat delicious charcoal grilled sardines.

What my friend did not refer to in this letter, but is obviously important, is that she and her husband have an occupation which not only is a major interest but adds to their income — writing and illustrating (with photographs) articles for English-language magazines and periodicals on agricultural and natural history subjects. 'We have no time for bridge or golf,' she says, 'although a golf course adjoins our garden, and our only extravagance is the buying of books and more and more shelves to put them on.'

Avoiding income tax and rates is an immense advantage if one lives abroad, and unlimited domestic help is available where this friend lives, though it is becoming more expensive, as is the cost of living. 'I love my countrymen,' she says, 'but if we lived in England I am afraid our standard of living would drop considerably — and the climate would have to change.' But this woman is one of the lucky ones. She could adapt to life in most countries, most places. 'I loved Japan (not Tokyo of course, but south somewhere), but alas it is the most expensive place in the world. I would not mind living in Brazil, or Australia, or perhaps Singapore, or, better still, in the south of

France where my brother lives. But isn't contentment in retirement something to do with the nature of the beast?'

I who am writing this book and those who read it may be sailing along, confident of being able to live in pleasant quarters of our own choice for many years. We may assume that some benign illness or accident will carry us off before we become a problem to ourselves or anyone else. But accidents happen, literally. After some small stumble which results in a broken limb we may become arthritic, or at least less mobile. We may be left on our own through the death of our partner, whether it is husband, wife, parent, son or daughter or home-sharing friend or relation. Then what? Living independently may not be easy then, and since it is a hazard we all face, it is well to know what some of the possibilities of local authority, housing association and charitable trust dwellings are like. The 'snapshots' which follow are all of homes for older people with which I happened to have some connection through friends, relations and neighbours, but they are by no means untypical.

The first development I visited is a moderate-sized block in a small town in the beautiful county of Derbyshire. It is a project of the West Derbyshire District Council and was opened to residents only in 1978. It is typical of the imaginative kind of provision for elderly couples and single people which was taking place all over the country in the 1970s. Victoria Court, as it is named, is not too large. There are sixty-four flats and flatlets, including two for the wardens and their families and two rooms for the residents' visitors, who pay only 58p a night, at the time of writing, for the simply furnished bedroom and bathroom. The architects made brilliant use of a hillside site, so that although there are five floor levels, all but the top one have direct access to a road. On each floor there are corner bays, looking out on the distant hills, where a table and comfortable chairs invite residents to sit and chat together and enjoy the fine views.

Victoria Court is what is called 'sheltered' housing, which means that the two resident wardens, both of whom are married with families, keep an eye on the flat dwellers. All residents have their own furniture, usually in an L-shaped room, which partly conceals the bedroom section from the view of visitors. There are built-in wardrobes, an excellent bathroom and a dream of a kitchen with fridge, cooking stove and cupboards as part of the fittings. The rent includes central heating and the flats are comfortably warm, but in very chilly weather, or for very elderly and skinny occupants, there are electric fires also — metered, so that the user pays the cost. I paid a visit to the Court in one of the coldest weekends of the winter of 1979, when it never stopped snowing for two days and the approaches from the road were practically impassable except for the very young and fit. The few residents who have cars could not get them out of their garages on to the road, and shopping was difficult. But the shops are, in fact, very near, and there is a good bus service to the centre of the busy little town.

From the wardens I learned that when the Court was first opened local people were rather reluctant to apply for the flats. They thought it looked a bit like a concentration camp — possibly because it has as a neighbour a small, modern factory, which it rather resembles in architectural style; possibly also because the long corridors are faced with 'stone' blocks, which have rather a prison-like aspect, and are carpeted with

28

sombre purple. But when the locals began to visit friends and relations there applications for flats quickly doubled, and there is now a waiting list. The flats are beautifully fitted up and must quickly feel homely. Most of the residents are in their sixties and early seventies, very active and well able to look after themselves. 'Wardening', however, is regarded as an essential ingredient of this type of accommodation. The focal point is the 'intercom' — a small panel in each flat and flatlet which is a telephone link to the wardens' flats. In each bathroom also there is a red cord which, when pulled, flashes on the wardens' control panels.

At Victoria Court one or other of the wardens rings round every flat at 8.55 a.m. to say 'Good morning. Did you have a good night?' Most of the residents have visiting family and friends, but for some the warden's voice may be the only greeting of the day. The wardens are not nannies or nurses, though. As in most sheltered housing, their duties are clearly laid down, and West Derbyshire's list of duties is worth quoting as typical.

The warden is expected:

To be alert to the degree of ill-health and dependence of each tenant and to take appropriate action whether through direct or indirect action to ensure that all is well with the person.

To make arrangements for answering emergency calls for the tenants for summoning the doctor or other services.

To give emergency help until local services and/or relatives can be summoned.

To maintain a record of the doctors and nearest relatives of each tenant and emergency telephone numbers.

To maintain a log-book or weekly report book.

To carry the responsibility of seeing that any service required by the tenant is sought as soon as possible, whether for medical, nursing, domestic or financial help.

To be responsible for the supervision of and security of the premises.

At Victoria Court there is no communal dining-room. Most tenants can manage their own shopping and cooking and enjoy it, even the single men, though some people have meals-on-wheels. The laundry room is well used, but the locker room where shopping can be left is less so, perhaps partly because the wardens deliver the mail — an unobtrusive way of keeping an eye on their flock. The wardens know they must not get too involved with the tenants' problems and affairs, but they do provide a listening-post and check frequently in person, rather than just by the intercom, on any tenant they think frail or exceptionally lonely. One of these wardens had been a deputy warden for some years before taking this full-time living-in post; the other had held various jobs in hospitals, so that both are well trained in 'caring'. They have two full days a week off, which means that for two days they each have to carry the other's duties as well as their own.

There does not seem to be very much visiting between tenants, though that may develop as they get to know one another better through the communal activities which the wardens organize. There is a large communal room which is quite inviting. Entertainment is chiefly of the bingo, whist, sing-song type, and though the wardens are energetic in their encouragement to tenants to participate, when I was there with them listening to an electric organ and percussion duo, they seemed reluctant to get off their chairs to dance. It was not so much that stiff knees and shortness of breath prevented these quite active people from joining in a dance or two I thought, as a reluctance to be *seen* dancing and 'carrying on'. One resident bravely sang two solos, with the organist, in a pleasant baritone and was warmly applauded. Perhaps others will gain enough confidence to do the same later, for there were obviously some quite good voices among the chorus of old-fashioned favourites.

There is, of course, a problem which the kindest and best-intentioned warden cannot easily solve. Tastes differ every bit as much in elderly people as in the young or the middle-aged. Bingo and sing-songs are the lowest common denominator, something everyone can join in — but not everyone wants to. Tenants whose interests have always been mildly intellectual cannot join in this kind of sociability without acute embarrassment as well as boredom. Perhaps in all such 'sheltered housing' developments efforts should be made to get the residents themselves to set up a fairly wide variety of 'entertainments' — certainly including classes, through either the local authority or the Workers' Educational Association or both. A mere handful of people is enough to set up a class in English literature, music appreciation, conversational French or fabric collage. Such classes would surely be the best way of developing the friendships which can be surprisingly lacking in sheltered accommodation. Our traditional reserve hardens when we are in a closed situation. ('Better not seem too friendly. If I find we haven't much in common, I don't want to be saddled with him or her dropping in all the while.')

Many English people, and perhaps also Welsh and Scottish people, are almost obsessively concerned to protect their privacy. People who have grown up at public schools or spent several years in the Forces may find this desire to protect their living-quarters from intrusion by outsiders difficult to understand. But it is surely obvious that the more crowded together people are, in the street, in the estate, in the flat block, the more they need to put an invisible wall round themselves. So do people who are housebound, especially if they are bedridden. Much as they may long for company, they often react very sharply against people who assume it is all right to pop in at any time without warning. To be a sitting target for neighbourliness is not as satisfactory as it may seem to the visitor.

British people who have travelled across America are often taken aback by the overwhelming sociability of the small township folk — so warm and outgoing that we tend to shrink right into our shells. The explanation needs only a moment's thought. America is a vast country. Around every little township there is an enormous, often uncultivated, open space. The newcomer is always a potential asset, not a threat. In our small, crowded islands the incomer is almost always initially resented, however hard he tries to be a good citizen and a good neighbour.

The Englishman's home is his castle. The trite old saying has lost very little of its potency. Being able to shut one's door firmly on the outside world can be a confirmation of one's status as a fully independent citizen, able to cock a snook at any one. This applies to youngsters in their first bed-sitter just as much as to the old. I remember very well the enormous satisfaction I felt in my first self-contained flat. To put my key in the lock, open the door into my private little world and slam the door after me was a superlative satisfaction. The elderly are all too apt to be 'invaded' by well-intentioned (indeed, often necessary) social workers and the like. Life in a 'colony' does not give quite the same feeling of privacy as life in a house in a street or a road. I was told of an elderly man who felt so passionately about his privacy that he persuaded the housing manager responsible for the block in which he lived to allow him to change his lock — with the result that not once but twice a warden had to summon help to break down the door when the tenant had had a fall and was in serious pain and unable to move.

The estate where this particular pensioner lives is a large development run by a 'housing trust for the aged'. The trust has a number of estates in Greater London and does not wish to be identified — like most housing trusts and associations — because of the fear of a rush of applications which it cannot satisfy. This trust retains firm control of the property though all the 'lets' are made through the local borough housing department. The wardens are responsible for informing the borough letting office of any expected vacancy and also for briefing new tenants about their rent and the conditions of residence. They also collect the rent weekly, in an office in the estate building.

Understandably, perhaps, this trust is apt to be a little more 'schoolmasterly' in its approach to tenants than a local authority might venture to be. I came upon a notice to tenants which warned them not to stub out cigarette ends or spit in the lifts: not to draw on the walls or in lifts or passages; not to leave the common room or TV room untidy; not to feed bread to the pigeons, 'as they foul the sills below, and the scraps may encourage rats and mice'. The trust also banned canvassing of the tenants after 8 p.m. during

33

the General Election of 1979 and laid down that individual candidates were not permitted to use the common room for meetings, though there might be a meeting addressed by all candidates if the sitting Member was willing to arrange it. Wardens were not allowed to deliver election addresses to tenants.

But despite this somewhat restrictive approach, the tenants I met were clearly pleased with their accommodation, thought it very good value and especially appreciated the kindly attitude of the wardens and their helpfulness in doing little errands, like collecting prescriptions for the housebound. All the tenants had their own well-fitted kitchens, but many took a mid-day meal (provided by the local authority) in the communal dining-room. The Women's Royal Voluntary Service often arranges this facility in local halls up and down the country — preferable, surely, to meals-on-wheels for all but the strictly housebound, since it provides company as well as food. Some of the estate tenants do have meals-on-wheels in their own flats.

In view of the fact that many of the estate's tenants must meet almost daily in the dining-room, there seems remarkably little 'neighbouring', probably even less than the tenants of Victoria Court in Derbyshire. Even a couple I met who were clearly sociable and public-spirited, helping to arrange outings, holidays and entertainments, said they were not in the habit of calling on their neighbours. The wardens here, kind and very hard-working as they were, seemed less involved in 'entertainment', possibly partly because the estate is very much bigger, and their day-to-day duties, like rent-collecting, more onerous. But I have a suspicion that the less *enclosed* an old people's 'colony' is, the less the residents are conscious of their neighbours, the less anxious they are to keep them at arm's length.

Certainly, I found a happily relaxed atmosphere in an estate in a lovely little old town in Sussex. The buildings are particularly elegant. Every flat has its white-painted balcony and the straight lines are broken by white-painted 'diamonds' on the upper floors. The lovely gardens are well stocked with roses and shrubs, and all the tenants look out on grass and trees. I had none of the 'shut-in' feeling here that some other flat blocks gave me. This estate is owned by a housing association which was started by half a dozen local people who wanted to provide homes for retired people. The only local authority housing, naturally enough, was for the lower-income groups, and in these beautiful southern counties there are many retired business and professional people, some of whom have lived there for years and others who moved on retirement to a slightly warmer climate and more agreeable surroundings.

The group registered itself as a housing association and then affiliated to the National Federation of Housing Associations. 'We had no money at all,' I was told, 'so we had to borrow the lot. The plans had to be approved by the Ministry [now the Department of the Environment] as well as by the District Council Housing Committee. We had many difficulties, but at last our plans were accepted and the Ministry agreed to our borrowing the whole of the money, about £500,000. It came via the local authority and has all to be paid back, with interest.' The association cannot charge rents higher than the local rent officer will permit, but otherwise has complete freedom in running the estate. In return for lending the money, the District Housing Committee has the right to recom-

mend 70 per cent of the tenants, and if the association's waiting is long, applicants will be advised to
put their names also on the council's list, if they live
in the district, to give them two chances. There is
always consultation over the acceptance of tenants.
'So far,' said my informant, 'we have accepted all their
names but one. There was a very good reason for not
admitting this person and the Housing Department
accepted our view.'

This estate is similar in size to Victoria Court —
seventy flats, two of which are occupied by wardens.
As is usual, some of the flats have separate sitting-
room and bedroom and some are bed-sitters. The
association was not allowed to build any with two
bedrooms and thinks this a pity. The official view is,
of course, that as many people should be housed as
the space and the money available will permit, but
for some retired people the move from a large three
or even four-bedroomed house would be easier if the
couple had an extra room which could double as a
spare room for visiting friends and family and a study,
hobby room or music room, even as a dining-room.
Many people find it difficult to get accustomed to
eating in the same room as they conduct all their
other activities. The estate has three quite delightful
guest rooms, which are very well used — no doubt
visiting the older members of the family is a treat in
such pleasant surroundings. The association also has
a smaller scheme, a house converted into thirteen units
and so in all houses more than a hundred retired
people.

There has always been support from the local
community. People have given donations, furniture,
garden tools, money for planting the gardens and so
on. But the next step, I was told, is 'to try to open

a small home for those who can no longer do their own shopping and cooking and looking after themselves, instead of having to go to a geriatric unit. For this we plan a drive to raise money.' Here we come to the crux of the provision of homes for people of retirement age. In all the developments started ten to fifteen years ago there was a substantial proportion of tenants, residents or whatever one calls them who went to live in their flats and bed-sitters when they belonged to the group I think of as the 'young-old' — less than seventy years old and able to contribute interest and activity to the community as well as needing very little support from it. By now most of those people are the 'old-old'. Many are over eighty, some over ninety. That does not prevent many of them from being in good nick, cheerful, busy, capable, well-friended — but, obviously some of the less lucky ones are frail physically and muddled mentally. In this group one may find the contankerous, bitchy and mean-spirited handful who can make the wardens' life a misery. I have been told stories of offensive and quite cruel verbal attacks on wardens and fellow residents. In the 'shut-in' atmosphere of some housing colonies, ill-feeling can breed like influenza germs. That it seldom causes real trouble is largely due to the tact and understanding of most wardens.

In the 'old-old' group one finds, of course, a few who are so vague that they forget they have turned the gas on, who lose their keys and their rent book and their essential papers. A few are incontinent or are arthritics so handicapped that they cannot bathe themselves or get in and out of bed unaided. So what happens to them? (We have to remember, without panic, that 'them' might include 'us'.)

No housing development for retired people can

provide fully for the casualties of old age, but the voluntary associations can and do concern themselves to provide 'refuges' to which those casualties can transfer, without too much misery for themselves or their families, when 'sheltered accommodation' with warden supervision is no longer enough. Wardens cannot undertake nursing. No tenant of a normal housing development can expect to stay in his independent flat if he cannot manage on his own. The geriatric unit, the nursing home, the hospice, is inevitable — but for such a small percentage of those of us who are now in our sixties that we can regard this much more as a problem we have to tackle for 'them' (like battered wives and babies, terminal cancers, spasticity and multiple sclerosis) than, in terror, as a prognosis of our own possible future.

We who own our own homes and are able still to live in them perhaps owe those who have not been so lucky an extra degree of concern. Some people — especially those whose lives have been spent mostly abroad — have never owned a home of their own; some, especially widows and single women, though also some elderly bachelors and widowers, have once had well-loved homes but have lost them through bereavement, change of job and so on. One of the happiest tenants of the Sussex housing estate is a longtime widow whose husband had been in the Indian police force. After his death she herself worked for some years abroad, with an association for the welfare of members of the Armed Forces, in India and the Middle East. When she finally returned to Britain she got what secretarial and clerking jobs she could and lived in a bed-sitter near Earls Court. 'Accommodation for single people is terribly difficult in London,' she said. 'I was getting desperate. It was really horrible where I was living, at the top of a house, with no entryphone, an absentee landlord and no caretaker. You didn't even hear the doorbell. I was often very nervous and had a jolly good chain on my door, for there were some very peculiar people living round about.'

This tenant was perhaps typical of the older women for whom housing ought to be provided by the community. Unable to find or to afford private accommodation, isolated, unhappy and nervous in 'bed-sitterland', they blossom in happier surroundings. Mrs X, who has no children of her own, has occasional visits from a niece and her husband and keeps in touch with a brother-in-law in Brighton and a friend in Worthing. Unlike the residents of some more 'enclosed' housing colonies, she calls in on neighbours for a cup of coffee and invites them back in return. 'I have a very kind neighbour', she says, 'who often invites me in to see a television programme as I have no set of my own.'

In another retirement home in the Home Counties, mainly for people associated with the stage, I met an unattached woman who said quite fiercely when I asked her if she was happy in her quarters, 'Yes, this is "*home*". I had a horrible time before, in a place where I had to share a bedroom with three other women. Their language was filthy and one was an alcoholic.' Sharing a bedroom with strangers can be trying at the best of times; if they are alien in their habits and ways of thinking, it must be hellish.

Many of the people who retire to 'colony' flats and flatlets are probably like Mrs X in the Sussex flats in being rather solitary and 'private' in their nature. She takes very little part in the entertainments organized by the tenants, though she will go, if asked, to a coffee morning. 'I am a quiet sort of person,' she says, 'and I don't really do anything much.' (Perhaps she needs quite a long while to regain energy after a rather hard and lonely life.) She reads a great deal and her other chief pleasure is solitary walking — in and around the hilly streets of the town, which at first made her legs ache but not now, and sometimes over the lovely Sussex Downs. We don't often think of *women* as solitary walkers, but some are. Just after meeting Mrs X I came upon a retired professional woman, living happily at home with her husband, who told me that *her* hobby was walking the Downs, setting off by train or bus and then walking nine or ten miles in the invigorating air.

Apart from local authority provision and local housing associations there are a good many houses and small estates run by charitable trusts, almshouses and similar historic establishments. The people who are able to spend their later days in such places are exceptionally fortunate, if the trust has money and can modernize and extend ancient buildings. Near my own home is a classic example of the beneficent trust, Morden College. It was designed by the greatest of all British architects, Sir Christopher Wren, in 1695. (Wren also designed the Astronomer Royal's house in nearby Greenwich Park, and a wall plaque says that it was not only for his convenience but 'a little for pompe'.) Morden College's history is fascinating. Daniel Defoe wrote of how the founder, Sir John Morden, told him that he had it in mind 'to make apartments for forty needy merchants . . . that as they had lived like gentlemen they might dye so'. Sir John was a city merchant-trader whose ships were thought to have foundered at sea, so that he experienced real poverty. When his fortunes improved this good man and his wife, who were childless, set about making provision for brother merchants and the like who had similarly met ill-fortune, so that they could end their days in decent comfort. Sir John's will of 1702 left his entire fortune in trust for the College, directing only that an annuity of £600 a year should be paid to his widow.

Most of the beneficiaries of almshouses and other establishments like Morden College have to fit into a certain category. In the case of Morden College, it was specified originally that they must be 'poor men of good character, either widowers or unmarried, at least 60 years of age, who shall have been merchants and shall have lost their estates by accident or misfortune in their honest endeavour to get their living by way of trading'.

Sir John Morden also directed that seven trustees should be chosen from the Turkey Company, of which he was a lifelong member, and if that company ceased to exist (as it did), from the Honourable East India Company, and if that should also come to an end, from the Court of Aldermen of the City of London. From 1884 the trustees have continued to be aldermen of the City of London, and by tradition every one of them has served a term as Lord Mayor. Sir John's intention to provide pleasant and dignified accommodation for 'failed merchants' has been carried through to our times, where the 'passport' to acceptance by the trustees for a vacancy is that the applicants should be 'poor men who shall have obtained rank or position of substantial authority in their employment, business or profession, and who are prevented from working by illness, accident or misfortune' (which is now interpreted to include old age). To us nowadays, 'College' is a misleading name, suggesting an educational institution. Its literal meaning is 'a body of colleagues', and what the colleagues unite for can be almost anything. The Collegium Musicum of London, for instance, is a group of singers who rehearse and perform oratorios and similar works. But the central quadrangle of Morden College has exactly the flavour of an Oxford college. The elderly single men who live in the forty-four apartments opening off a pillared cloister round a lovely square of grass and flower beds are indeed privileged. From their front doors they can rest their eyes on the elegant lamp standards and the ponds with their goldfish and water lilies. These tenants are called 'members of the College', unlike the tenants of the other, newer buildings, who are 'resident beneficiaries'. The 'members' lunch together in a fine, handsome dining-room just as if they were Oxbridge dons dining 'in hall'. This dining-room was added to the original building in 1844, but it is entirely in the Wren architectural tradition.

Morden College might have continued to house only two or three score of elderly gentlemen but for the fact that Sir John Morden was a shrewd and far-sighted businessman. He purchased the freehold of the Manor of Old Court, 230 acres mainly along the banks of the Thames between Greenwich and Charlton. When Sir John bought this land it was marsh, producing small grazing rents and flooded in winter, but now, having long since been drained, it is covered with houses, factories, warehouses and office blocks, so that the Morden College estate has become well funded by the ground rents of many fine and valuable properties in Blackheath and Greenwich — like the Paragon crescent, which is one of the outstanding features of Blackheath's interesting architecture.

From 1871 the College has had 'non-resident pensioners', who get grants to help them to stay on in their own homes or to pay for accommodation in private residential homes. In 1908 widows and single women were included among these out-pensioners. But after the Second World War the trustees realized that the College had sufficient funds to put up more buildings in the spacious grounds. The change in the climate of opinion about housing the elderly was no doubt the spur. In 1951 thirty-two flats for married couples were built in a two-storey block, each with its own little garden. Six years later a similar block for twelve married couples was opened, and then came the first block to provide domestic and light nursing care. Of the twenty-five residents in this block, sixteen received this kind of help.

And so to the essential last step: the trustees had a block designed and built for the really old and frail, women as well as men, who need full nursing care. It was realized that the healthy and lively 'young-old' who take up quarters at the College inevitably become, if they survive, the 'old-old'. This process may take ten or even twenty years, but that is quite long enough to put down roots as strong and deep as in the happy family home of earlier days. Indeed, for some people, such as missionaries and others who have always worked abroad, this may be the only settled home they have ever had. How cruel to turn them out, to force them or their families — if they have any — to find a bed in a geriatric ward in a strange place among strange and perhaps unlikeable people. If the move to a nursing unit can be made within the 'colony', where they will have made at least pleasant acquaintances, if not close friends, and where the majority of people are interested and interesting, their chances of a comfortable last phase of life are very much higher. This is an aspect of residential provision that needs much thought and discussion.

When people apply for residence at Morden College they are expected to make a full statement of their financial situation. If they are 'elected', they are told what 'contribution' is expected of them, according to their means. This 'contribution' entitles them to breakfast in their rooms and lunch — in hall for the exceptionally fortunate 'members' — or in the dining-rooms of the different 'courts'. For supper they can either take a light meal in their own quarters or patronize the snack bar in the excellent club room, which has also a drinks bar. The residents have a work-shop where they can do woodwork, pottery, weaving and other crafts. An occupational therapist pays weekly visits. There are also bowling greens, a putting course and a croquet lawn in the beautifully main-tained grounds. A College doctor pays regular visits, and a resident chaplain (a retired local vicar) takes daily services in the chapel, which was consecreated by the Bishop of Rochester in 1702. There is also a library, with archives of great interest and historical value.

The College is run beneficently rather than demo-cratically, and there is a strange anachronism in the 'election' of women as 'resident beneficiaries'. Appli-cants from women tend to be considered primarily on the ground that they are the widows of men possessing the required qualifications, or elderly unmarried daughters, 'where it can be shown they have given up the chance of a home and a life of their own to look after elderly parents'. So retired heads of schools, doctors, matrons, lawyers, accountants and business executives may have to look elsewhere for homes in their later years if they have the misfortune to have been born female!

Peter Townsend's excellent book about housing for the elderly, to which I have already referred, is most unfortunately titled *The Last Refuge.* The place in which one lives from sixty onwards is no more a 'refuge' than the place in which one lives from forty to sixty, unless one is ill, or mentally or physically disabled, or for any reason confined to bed. But there *is* that minority, and it needs the community's care and concern. Unfortunately, the very old who are physically and mentally incapacitated are at the very bottom of the pile when it comes to finding people willing to look after them. This was explained to me: 'With children or young people, even if they are gravely physically or mentally handicapped, there is hope of improvement, even if it comes very slowly and is not very great. With old people there is almost always bound to be a further decline.' (This is not absolutely true. There are many instances of people who have declined when taken into geriatric units but have made astonishing progress towards participation in daily life when they have been transferred to a more relaxed and supportive atmosphere.)

There are, one is thankful to report, dedicated people willing to serve the needs of perhaps the least attractive section of the community and other good people willing to work to raise the money to establish homes where the very old and afflicted can live out their last days in a serene and peaceful atmosphere. Philip Godlee Lodge, in one of Manchester's pleasantest suburbs, is such a place. It was set up as a memorial to a local citizen who had been a leading figure in musical and social service enterprises. The Lodge is a beautiful old house, every room looking on to equally beautiful grounds. Here live forty-six very old women, mostly 'incapable' through physical disabilities or mental deterioration. Most are unable to walk, or unable to communicate, or unable to get out of bed or dress themselves without help. The patient/ staff ratio is one to one. When I was there, one sunny spring afternoon, the television was bumbling on in the sitting-room. The faces that were turned towards the set registered no animation, yet one had the strong feeling that it would be missed if someone were to switch off, just as the sunlit lawns and trees would be missed if the curtains were drawn.

What does life hold for these pathetic survivors? Their daily needs are met as well as any loving son or daughter could hope — at a cost to the community of £83 a week in 1979. The residents pay nothing themselves, but their pensions are reduced to £2 a week. Referrals to Philip Godlee Lodge are by the consultants at the two largest Manchester hospitals, Crumpsall and Withington, covering the north and the south sides of the city. The original aim, to provide short-stay accommodation for the old and infirm, to give their families a break, has been practically given up. So has the admission of male patients. This is because the demand for permanent-stay beds in this kind of accommodation is so heavy.

Life is not all monotony. An occupational therapist comes once a week, and quite a few of the residents enjoy learning to do things with their hands. Many make small items like covers for coat-hangers. Possibly the best therapy is provided by the matron, an elegant woman with a sense of style who handles the patients' banked pensions for them. She buys not only smart slippers but rather splendid gowns and perfume for Christmas. A hairdresser comes weekly, and these

46

very old ladies, despite their sometimes vacant or morose expressions, never look decrepit or even dowdy.

The Area Health Authority now pays the Lodge's running costs and repairs, but capital costs have to be raised by charitable efforts. £6,000 was raised for a chapel of rest and amenities like glassing in the veranda. The management committee would now very much like to raise sufficient money for an extension with twenty-six more beds, for the area is desperately short of accommodation of this tender, supportive and non-institutionalized kind. When I visited Philip Godlee Lodge the committee did not think the times propitious for fund-raising, though why, one wonders, when the need is so compelling?

A visit to a home for incurables in south London emphasized some of the same thoughts with considerable force. Though this a huge mansion, with corridors almost as wide as a street and beautiful big dayrooms, where the patients also take their meals together, there are four beds to a room. Does it have to be so? How does it feel, when one is half-paralysed or confined to bed or even to a wheelchair, to have to share every moment of one's life with strangers? (This very often applies equally to very expensive private homes.) Does one lose all sensitivity to the presence of others when one is very old and infirm? Or does gratitude for being cared for in one's distress drive out all irritation or resentment? And what can the community do about it, anyway, in these days of insistence on 'cuts in public spending'?

There is no doubt that residental care of the old and frail has come on impressively since the end of the Second World War, but I don't believe we have got it quite right yet and suggest that it is up to those of us who, because of our years, are coming close to the problem to stir up discussion — and action where possible. It is not 'right' for us to have to share a bedroom with four strangers or a lounge with forty. It is not 'right' for us to be stranded miles away from family, friends and associates in a geriatric ward. It is not 'right' for most of us to be segregated by age from the rest of the community. The 'right' way for most of us to live is the way we have always lived, in a mixed-sex, mixed-age community.

3
People

People need people. The human race could not have survived if we hadn't learned that. Even St Simeon Stylites on his pillar, even the English tramp and the Burmese monk, for ever on the road, are as dependent on other people to give them food and drink as the newborn infant. We often say that we aim to bring up our children to be independent adults — but in fact *interdependent* is what we mean. We aim to socialize them, to enable them to relate to other people, first to siblings and parents, then to school-mates, so that later they can become integrated with adult society. Relating to other people is the dominant pattern of our lives.

It is often forgotten that this pattern can be pulled askew and even totally disrupted by retiring, or being retired, from our work, because it tends to be based on a network of relationships centering on our employment. This is especially true for those of us who live in commuterland, for even colleagues who have been rather more than pleasant companions tend to drop quite quickly out of our lives if visiting means a ten-mile journey and if our married partners have not been used to socializing together. Retirement can be all too like bereavement. Husbands' friends, say widows, soon disappear from the scene. So often do work friends, unless there is a bond other than simply the job and the workplace.

To be known, to be recognized, to be greeted — for most of us this is what makes us a real person in our own eyes. To be anonymous for a little while is very pleasant if one has had too much responsibility for people in one's working life. But not for ever. To be anonymous in a community where all the other people seem to know one another, to become the faceless outsider, is disconcerting and can even be traumatic.

I had an insight into this disconcerting experience when I attended the centenary celebrations at my old school. It had never occurred to me before that because the label pinned on my dress would mean absolutely nothing to the people milling around me — I had moved out of my usual milieu — I should feel like one of those sea creatures whose fronds cast around in the water until they find a rock or a shell to adhere to. Obviously, I have become too accustomed to being known to at least one or two people in most places I frequent. It was salutary to have to accept that I am validated, so to speak, by the people with whom I associate.

That story of the man who fell out of a train in the middle of Europe, without passport, wallet or any other means of identification, has always frightened me. He had become a non-person. How totally destructive of personality it must be to have no points of reference in your life. If nobody knew me, if I were like those poor souls who doss down in derelict buildings and under arches, I think I should cease to have any meaning to myself. One fears it could be like that for people who not only are severed from their workplace, but sever themselves from their familiar surroundings. No one knows them. They are truly face-less.

Of course, for people whose workplace and home are not far apart and whose work life and leisure life are quite closely integrated, this aspect of ageing is not nearly so difficult. The favourite pub, with its cluster of like-minded cronies, is still accessible, and the interests of the community can quite naturally, and almost inevitably, become more important than the former commitment to the workplace. So the most important element in deciding where to live as one grows older is whether there will be a circle of friends available. It is often said, and regarded as proven, that the older one grows, the harder it is to make friends. I have not found this to be true, and see no reason why it need be true for other people. When people share a common interest — unless it is football, tennis or any other sport demanding tip-top physical strength and control — age is remarkably unimportant. This is certainly true of music, drama and painting, where the age range of those working together may be from twenty to eighty or more. Anyone who has been to a summer school of music will probably have observed a string quartet in which the second violin may be a boy in his twenties and the cello a woman in her seventies. A common cause is as good for friend-making as a shared hobby. I have a treasured photograph of three women walking together to lobby MPs in support of an anti-discrimination Bill. One was ninety-plus, one forty-plus and one twenty-plus.

One hopes, indeed, to take a few friends along from school days until one's last years. They are a delight to talk to, for they are like family — nothing needs to be recapitulated, nothing explained. But one is bound to lose a few contemporaries along the way, and the man or woman who has not replaced them with younger people with common interests is going to find ageing increasingly lonely. Isn't the *family* enough then? It may be, if it is large, close-knit and long-lived. But brothers and sisters do not always live near at hand. Some marry people we do not like. Some, like school friends, die untimely. In later years family gatherings become fewer. First it is weddings, then christenings — and then, alas, funerals. We are indeed lucky if we still have an older brother or sister to tease us and prevent us from getting cocky. In a close family, too, there are usually affectionate nieces and nephews whom one has known all their lives who will keep alive the vital sense of 'belonging', either out of genuine feeling or out of a profound sense of family duty, which still is a factor in many family lives.

There are people who despise or dislike the 'blood tie', people who say, 'You *choose* your friends. Why should you have to put up with your family if you don't like them?' I am one of the people who think that blood may indeed by thicker than water, because even across the Atlantic I have recognized family likenesses which may very well indicate more than a mere facial resemblance. But even if this is self-deception, I think that the *assumption* that families should stick together and support one another in times of trouble is still a pretty reliable insurance against isolation in later years, even if it is no more than 'Oh, gosh, I ought to do something about poor Aunt Mabel.'

But what about our own children as the last insurance we can have against an isolated old age? Statistically, about a third of people over retirement age have no children. *A third!* How bleak life is likely to be for them in their later years unless they have taken the trouble to maintain a link with nieces and nephews, godsons and goddaughters and other young people met through various work and leisure interests. I have a friend who has at least eight godchildren. I expect some are now parents, and so my friend has another generation of children coming along to concern herself with. Isn't that a splendid way to live? But what about the 66 per cent of us who do have children and, probably, grandchildren? Aren't they going to satisfy our need for younger company? Perhaps; perhaps not. In this shrunken world in which we live our children may well be living in North America, South America, Africa or Australia. I have, in fact, two friends whose only grandchildren live in Vancouver and whose other offspring have not married. I have another friend whose first grandchild was taken to Congo when he was scarcely a year old and who now lives with his parents, his brother and his sister in Switzerland.

Sons and daughters, we agree, have to go their own way. They do not now think of it as their duty to give up their way of life to stay where they can keep their ageing parents company. And which of us elderly persons would now put pressure on them to stay when they long to go? We parents bring up our children in the hope that they will become good citizens. When they are ready to go we must wave them on their way — and if they come back, asking for help and assuming it is their natural right to get it, we must shrug our shoulders and do the best we can. That's life.

It is quite impossible to generalize about family relationships. Some women dote on their mothers-in-law. So do some men. Some mothers, fathers, sons, daughters, daughters-in-law and sons-in-law meet together in perfect harmony and even live together.

Many young women, in my experience, get on famously with their father-in-law, especially if he has no daughter, or if his daughter has moved far away. Many fathers and sons-in-law get on famously if they share a hobby, like being a radio ham (sometimes even to the exclusion of the unlucky young wife). But every one of these relationships can be bitterly unhappy and stressful to both generations. You don't have to worry too much about people you can't get on with, unless they are related to you or connected by marriage. In that case you have to make a strenuous effort to establish a tolerable relationship for the sake of the members of the family whom you dearly love. What one hopes, of course, is to keep a loving relationship with one's own children, with the men and women they marry and with the grandchildren whom they produce. All too often this is easier said than done. One can give no advice, only say that it is wise not to risk putting any strain on the ties of relationship and usually to keep a reasonable distance, emotionally if not literally. This is no simple matter, for the daughter (or daughter-in-law) who has made it very clear that she wants to live her own life, with minimal contact with parents or parents-in-law, may suddenly ask for, even demand, help with the grandchildren, expecting that they should be taken over at short notice, even at considerable inconvenience, if she has to go into hospital or wishes to start a new job or go to Tokyo on a business trip with her husband. It may be hard for Granny to swallow her wave of resentment but, for the sake of her future valued relationship with the little ones, she had better say 'yes'. For most of us grandparents – grandfathers as well as grandmothers – the children are what makes parenthood all worthwhile: those long-ago nights walking the bedroom with a squalling baby, and those more recent nights listening in fear for the sound of a beloved teenage daughter's latchkey in the front door.

When a son or daughter takes a partner who is anathema to us, and whom we can scarcely tolerate in our home, husbands and wives have to give one another a lot of support. Bear it. Don't protest. If we shut the door on that wretched man (or woman) we shall amost inevitably lose our son/daughter and our grandchildren as well.

Even sadder is the conflict that can grow between mother and grown-up daughter, father and grown-up son. I have met quite a few women who have made no bones about 'hating' their mother. I have met even more elderly women who are hurt and bewildered because their daughters seem to dislike and despise them. A letter in the feminist magazine *Spare Rib* a year or two ago asked, 'Why do our daughters seem to hate us so? Why even if they are "fond" of us do they think so poorly of us?' 'Recently,' the writer continued, 'a woman told me that she had invited her parents to a gathering. When she told her friends this they opted not to come. "If you've invited your parents you can't expect us to come too." On another occasion this woman had attended a women's conference and gone into a workshop on "motherhood". As she sat down two younger women walked to the door, one saying, "I'm not going to stay here if a woman of that age is going to listen to everything I say." ' She summed up: 'Something has happened to make the daughters of some of the most active and independent women the world has ever known feel that their mothers are shameful and foolish . . . and the mothers acquiesce in this.' What else can we do, I wonder, but acquiesce? Perhaps we sowed the seeds of this attitude when our children were young, by refusing to be authoritarian? Parents with daughters like this just have to find reassurance among their contemporaries. They will find sympathetic ears, without a doubt.

Perhaps successful sons cut their retired fathers down to size in a similar way. I wouldn't know about that. But I do know that men as well as women can find an undreamed of joy in their retirement years through their grandchildren, whose company and uncritical love add a dimension to life that was scarcely possible in earlier, more crowded and stressful years. Grandparents, of course, can be ideal baby-sitters, not grumbling at being kept up after midnight, not expecting payment, ready and willing at almost all times and, of course, trustworthy and acceptable to the children themselves. There is more to it than that, though. Grandparents have more time and patience than parents. Do you remember how impatient you were with your own children when they insisted on walking along every wall on your way to the shops, or on pushing their own pushchair? You were always in a hurry. Now, in retirement, you are not, and the antics of the toddlers are endearing rather than frustrating. Granny is happy to teach little Jenny how to do cross-stitch or to make fudge with her. Grandpa is willing to throw and catch for Johnny for very much longer than he was with his own son, or to play dominoes or draughts or even that supremely boring card game variously named 'Strip Jack Naked', 'Drain the Well Dry' or 'Beggar My Neighbour'.

If you live near enough, you can be the person the shy child asks to help with maths or spelling when she is scared of being laughed at at school, or the person who won't get out of patience with the cocky little boy who wants to brag about how many runs he made or goals he scored. And children hug and kiss. If you are left on your own by the death of your life-time partner, your grandchildren are literally the only human beings to whom you can show physical affection — kiss, cuddle, take into your bed or your bath. They may seem to be the sole reason for wanting to go on living.

Even in this sweetest of relationships there are hazards, of course. The more the child puts his/her trust in you, the more you must be discreet. Never pass on to the parents what the child has told you; never allow the parents to imagine that you are likely to assume an undue share of the child's affection; never criticize the parents' handling of their children, even when you disapprove or when you sympathize with the child's occasional grouses against the parents. You have a loyalty both to your own child and to your grandchild, and sometimes it may be necessary to remind the grandchild, 'I don't think you ought to behave like that to your Mummy/Daddy. He/she is *my* little boy/girl, and I am on his/her side.' Perhaps sometimes we could say what I used to say to my own daughter when she was young and rebellious and we were not getting on very well: 'Well, we are stuck with one another, you and I, like it or not. We had better try to cope as well as we can.'

Indeed, in the difficult late-teenage years grandparents who are trusted both by their sons and daughters and by their grandchildren can be a help in difficult situations. A friend of mine was able to be the confidante of a granddaughter who eloped to the Continent with a married man and could not bring herself to discuss the situation with her parents. The girl's mother was thankful that her own mother, a calm, dispassionate, uncensorious woman, was able to be the link between the girl and her anxious parents. A distraught parent *can* sometimes say to a distraught young person, 'I *know* you can't tell me what it is that you are in such a state about. But don't you think you could tell Granny (or even Grandfather)?'

A very sad problem for grandparents, now growing quite common, is that the divorce of their offspring may deprive them, as well as the actual parent, of access to the beloved child or children. No one who has not experienced it can know the anguish of the grandparents, as well as of the parent, at the decision of a court to award custody of the children to a hostile in-law. Grandparents have no standing in these tragic custody cases. They cannot stand up in court and say to the judge, 'The child is our child too, blood of our blood, flesh of our flesh, our hope for the future. If you punish our child by refusing custody to him/her, you punish us too.'

Yet in this tussle for the *love,* not only the custody, of the child, the grandparents may after the first bitter grief has lessened, be able to help the child, even if not the deprived parent. It is a little easier for grandparents to see that the only victory worth winning in the battle between the parents is the emotional stability of the child. They can talk to the child more reasonably and help him/her to cope with divided loyalties, to believe that both parents love him/her, and that this genuine love is at least part of the reason for the tug o'war.

I tend, naturally, to write as a grandmother, but no one should suppose that grandfathers are not equally concerned with grandchildren and do not equally enjoy their company. Quite often when I am out shopping I see retired men taking toddlers for a walk in their pushchairs, or even pushing prams. My father dearly loved his first granddaughter (he did not live to see his second); my father-in-law's big moment of the day was when my little daughter climbed on to the back of his chair at bedtime and kissed his bald head. My husband was equally enchanted by our first grand-daughter and she loved her 'Pa Pa', whom she dimly recalls, although he died when she was two and a half. Men who have not had much time for grandparenting during their working life may have an enchanting surprise when more free time enables them to share in the developing verbal and physical skills of the very young.

It is fairly certain that though your sons and daughters may find you boring, your grandchildren will not. It seems to me that some sons and daughters need to extend to their parents the courtesy that they would show to other guests and draw them into the conversation round the dinner table, otherwise parents tend to dry up totally and become really a dead loss, the sort of guests one doesn't invite again.

But it is useless to deny that there is a real risk of becoming a bore in one's retired years — partly because one is liable to take in fewer experiences, fewer thoughts which can be digested and can form the subject of stimulating converstation. It is an aspect of later life that we all ought to question ourselves about. Everyone writes as if only other people were boring. Indeed, bores, poor things, seem sometimes to justify their existence by providing a chance for clever people to shine at their expense. I suspect that even the wittiest people can be boring some of the time and to some of the people they meet, especially if they give way to the temptation to hog the show. 'Anecdoters' are probably most in danger of becoming bores, and I suspect they may include me, for I am liable to react to certain stimuli with the same story. If someone starts, for instance, on the confusion between similar surnames, I tend to tell the story of how I used to be confused with Mary Stocks (the Baroness Stocks of the Royal Borough of Kensington and Chelsea) after *she* had stopped being confused with Marie Stopes. I *think* that most of the anecdotes I produce almost automatically in response to stimuli, just as if someone had put a penny in a slot, are quite entertaining, and they do usually raise a laugh; I *think* I avoid the trap of telling the same stories over again in the same company. But can I be sure? Shall I go on being careful about the audience? Shall I grow increasingly garrulous with the years? And is there any one other than myself I can rely on to stop me if I am in real danger of turning into a bore? Yet if I do stop telling my little stories, out of fear of slipping into anecdotage, am I not equally in danger of becoming a bore by reason of having nothing entertaining to contribute to the conversation?

The dilemma is not easy to resolve, but I think we can grasp a guideline or two. Guideline No.1 is summed up in a delightful text hanging on the wall in an office of Age Concern's headquarters at Bernard Sunley House, Mitcham. It is said to be a seventeenth-century nun's prayer and reads: 'Keep me from the fatal habit of thinking I must say something on every subject and on every occasion.' Guideline No. 2 is that though your nears and dears do not want to hear your reminiscences, 'olden times' (which means anything before the Second World War) can be of fascinating interest to the very young. Men who fought in either world war should not regard that as licence to go on talking about it for ever (nor should their wives, who served in the ATS, made munitions or did fire-watching), but these times can be of stirring interest to younger people who cannot imagine what it was like to be in a plane dropping bombs over Dortmund, or in Coventry, listening to the wail of the sirens and the nerve-tautening drone of the enemy planes, the bark of the anti-aircraft guns and the sinister slither of masonry that followed the horrendous explosion of the bomb. The Second World War is history-book stuff now, and we who remember it so clearly can illuminate it in a way no history book can. An African student recently told me how grateful he was to an elderly East End couple who told him what life was like under saturation bombing. (He never guessed how grateful they probably were to him for encouraging them to talk!)

Guideline No. 3 is that conversation is a to-and-fro. I don't think anyone is in serious danger of being a bore who is meticulous about throwing a lead back to the other person. Taking part in radio discussions has been a good discipline for me in this way. Two or three sentences, and then you toss a ball to your partner. But perhaps we should all, as we grow older, keep a surreptitious account of the number of sentences *we* contribute to a conversation compared with the other people. Or perhaps we should keep a tally stick in the wardrobe and cut a notch every time we tell a favourite anecdote? It might be rather a startling sight at the end of a year.

Couples who move into their sixties and seventies, still happy to be together after thirty or forty years of marriage, should not have many 'people' problems. When there is always a 'friend in the house' to talk things over with, even major griefs become bearable. The intolerance or patronage of one's offspring —

61

which is really role reversal, the child behaving as if he/she were the parent — can be turned into a shared joke. There is no fear of loneliness, and there is always the possiblity of talking over what is going on in the world and the comfort of having a partner to share decision-making about practical matters, such as changing from coal fires to gas fires or whether central heating can be afforded.

This sharing of concern and, hopefully, of responsibility for the running of a home and the ordering of one's life pattern is a boon and a blessing which people do not always appreciate — until one partner is removed from the scene, too often by death, but sometimes (and more often than one would expect) by divorce. To those of us who are, or who have been, happily married for a great many years, the notion of divorce at the sort of age at which men normally retire is startling. But increasingly, so a woman divorce lawyer told me, it is happening. In my young days divorce was an unthinkable disgrace for a woman, however virtuous she was and however guilty her husband. I had an aunt whose husband treated her abominably. Her sisters, my mother and another aunt, did their utmost to persuade her to leave him. She was a trained teacher and so could have maintained herself, and there were no children. But my poor aunt felt that any kind of husband was better than none and was a guarantee of status and respect in the society in which she lived. She never left him, and two years after he died, mercifully in our eyes, she died too. A sad story which could hardly happen today, for divorce now is not disgraceful, and people of any age can divorce by consent after living apart for two years, or sue for divorce after five years apart even if the other partner is not willing. Good people like the late Lady Summerskill opposed this legislation on the ground that it was a 'Casanova's Charter' and would enable men to discard their faithful wives of many years and go off with attractive younger women. That is not, in fact, what has happened to any great extent. In many cases of late divorce it is the wife who is utterly fed up with her partner and who is, surprising as it may seem, encouraged by her grown-up sons and daughters, to get rid of him.

My lawyer friend said, 'You get the wife who has been downtrodden for most of the marriage. As the couple are moving towards retirement, she realizes how much she has been under her husband's thumb and she gets itchy feet. The married sons and daughters are likely to say to her, "For goodness sake, you have put up with this for all these years. Break away now, while you are still young enough to enjoy your free-dom."' And once an elderly women has made up her mind that she wants her freedom, she wants it *now.* It is, said my friend, only the younger people who tend to say, 'We'll separate for two years and then divorce by consent.' If there is bad feeling in marriage, it gets worse with the years and late divorce can be astonishingly bitter — especially, probably, to the man who has gone his own selfish way for years and cannot imagine that his life partner may decide to stop being a doormat for him just as he is coming up to retirement and counting on all home comforts.

The selfish husband may have a severe financial shock, too. Once a wife is divorced she can draw her retirement pension at the age of sixty even if her husband has not reached the pensionable age of sixty-five. She counts as a single woman and gets the benefit of her husband's social security contributions right up to the day the decree is made absolute. After that she is assessed for a single person's pension — much more than she would have got if still married. What is more, a woman's rights in the matrimonial home are likely to have priority over the man's and a judge is quite likely to decide that the wife must have the home if she has no other possibility of suitable accommodation and the husband has. (Men have the same security of tenure if they apply for a divorce and the property is in the wife's name.)

But being fed up with a rather one-sided matrimonial bargain, as I think many older women are, isn't necessarily a guarantee that one will be happier alone. I am certain that middle-aged sons and daughters should be very cautious about advising Mum to break free. A letter to the retired people's newspaper *YOURS* said, 'My father and mother have been married for forty-five years and I believe they have been years of hell for Mum.' Apparently the writer's father always drank heavily and tended to knock his wife about. In later years he was drinking less and was less violent, but still spent most of his time in the pub and kept his wife very short of money. The writer asked the advice columnist of *YOURS* whether she should persuade her mother to leave and to make her home with her daughter. The columnist was very cautious in her advice. So would I be. So was I cautious when discussing with the psychologist Dr Wendy Greengross on a BBC *Woman's Hour* programme the scores of letters from women disenchanted with marriage, frustrated and miserable in late middle age and looking for a way out. Being on your own after many years of being half of a partnership, even a fairly unsatisfactory partnership, is a very shaking experience. Should there not be trial separations for couples who are not comfortable together, and who secretly or overtly dread that retirement will mean being thrown into one another's company for all their waking hours, every day, every week, every month of their lives? I have been told a few sad stories of stress suffered by *wives* in this situation. Husbands should be aware of this risk.

A friend of mine, blessed with adequate capital, bought herself a house in the country and got enormous satisfaction out of doing it up and laying out the garden. Her husband stayed on in the marital home near London. There has never been any urge on either side to sue for divorce. Occasionally they visit one another. There are occasional family gatherings with the daughters. So long as they do not share a home they get on quite well. Obviously, money has eased this situation, but a frank acceptance of it has eased it still more. It is not impossible, as so many older women seem to think, to maintain oneself for a while — as a canteen cook, a supermarket check-out lady, a saleswoman in a shoe shop. 'What, *me*? I have a degree in history', or 'I was a nurse or a primary school teacher', or 'I did market research or was in charge of a laundrette.' So what? A woman who is contemplating leaving her husband and setting up on her own has to be able and willing to stand on her own feet, which means by definition that she must be able and willing to earn her own living, at whatever job turns up.

Men and women who seriously consider breaking up an unsatisfactory relationship when retirement makes it possible for both to go their own ways, supported by state pensions, should pause for long, long thought. Think of having to say, possibly for ever more, 'I' instead of 'we'. Think about loneliness. Perhaps you don't know about that, as bereaved and divorced and deserted men and women know? As I know. You, who have lived thirty or forty years as half of a pair, go to the pub, or to a women's meeting, or to bingo, or to the gramophone society, where most of the people present are half of a pair, and you go home to an empty house. You are *alone*; you have no one to sound off to, no one to discuss with, no one even to say goodnight to. That's when you begin to know about loneliness. It is ridiculous for people to be lonely, you may say, from the security of your marital partnership, your multitude of friend-producing interests. Little you know. Death, desertion, disaster at work or in personal life may totally destroy your confidence in yourself. Loneliness is a creeping paralysis of the social responses. If one doesn't recognize this, one will end up like the old lady who wrote in her diary, day after day, 'Nobody came', or the old man in the 'sheltered' flat who barred his door, literally, against any visitor, however concerned and well intentioned.

Social intercourse rests on the assumption that you are quite pleased to see me, I am quite pleased to see you, and even if we are fairly indifferent to one another, the pretence is a useful social insurance and not really unpleasant. We chat on, out shopping, walking the dog, going to collect the pension, saying 'Good morning' to an acquaintance or two, not really involved, but not for a moment wondering whether our presence is boring or a nuisance. If Mrs A or Mr B calls out as we pass, 'Good morning. Sorry I can't stop,' we take it at its face value. But the psychologically lonely take it as an intentional slight and are convinced that it indicates a distaste for their company. The socially secure aren't much bothered even if they do think that Mrs A is deliberately avoiding them. There will always be Miss B or Mr C. The socially secure don't expect *everyone* to welcome their company. The psychologically lonely take every apparent rebuff as an indication that they are virtually leprous.

Probably at least 80 per cent of us have social assurance and take social intercourse so much for granted that we can't explain to the truly lonely how we put out acceptable signals, just as with a girl I knew at school who asked me to explain to her how I knew that when I opened my mouth a certain note would come out. I couldn't explain; she couldn't understand. Our social assurance is more precarious than most of us think. It may be destroyed by the death of a beloved life partner, the brutal end of a love affair, the break-up of marriage or the loss of a job not only through redundancy, but through enforced and deeply reluctant retirement. It is after a shock like this that being alone is apt to stop being an oasis in an overcrowded life and becomes *being lonely* – shut in with one's own not very likeable self, self-doubting, self-pitying, inert, broody, suspicious and eventually hostile to the outside world.

With most of us, mercifully, this kind of psychological illness runs its course and clears up, like influenza, only like pneumonia, a bit more threatening for the elderly – who may lack the stimulus of work and work colleagues – than for those still fully employed. But, like cancer, it is almost certainly not incurable if caught in time. The sort of things one says about loneliness can sound pretty silly to those who have never been afflicted by it and pretty intolerant to those who are. I think it is feeble and selfish to give way to loneliness if one is in reasonable health, mobile and literate in a world full of lonely people who would be glad of a hand. But if creeping paralysis of the social responses hadn't got a hold and weren't a psychological illness for which no one should be blamed, there wouldn't be a loneliness problem, would there?

Writing a book about ageing one wants to stress always the satisfactions and opportunities retirement can bring, but it would be wrong to run away from the sad fact that one half of every married couple will die before the other half. Bereavement of this kind doesn't only mean loneliness of the most devastating kind, but a wilderness of pain and desolation impossible to imagine beforehand or to protect oneself against. I have no doubt at all that grief is a psychological illness which can have strange, quite severe physical manifestations — unaccountable aches and pains, or failure of the senses and even the limbs to function properly.

One can help only a very little by talking about this saddest of human predicaments. If you are bereft, accept that you have to trudge through each day as it comes, thankful when it is over and hoping for nothing better the next day or the day after. Remember that millions of others have been through this intolerable experience and survived, even if just now you yourself have no wish to survive. However unlikely it seems now, there may still be a point in going on living. So do what is asked of you, accept kindly meant invitations, summon all your strength to fight self-pity and *do* something, preferably practical and undemanding, as soon as you have the strength and the will power. (A curious occupation I found for myself was to spend night after night white-washing the cellar. It did help.)

If it is your brother, sister or dear friend who is

bereaved, don't just invite him/her round for coffee or a meal, though that is usually helpful, especially if you can gently encourage the bereaved one to talk, even to weep. Ask him or her to *do* something for you, or for some concern you are interested in. Nothing too much, for most of us have precious little energy in the first months, but something that will be a commitment. The worst thing about bereavement is the overwhelming sense of the futility of one's existence, and many elderly widows and widowers are a serious suicide risk for some months after their partner's death.

There is *no* preparation that any of us can make for coping with the effect of the loss of a life partner, for one simply does not know and cannot imagine what one's reactions will be, but it does seem the most obvious common sense for people on the doorstep of retirement to consider together, with good humour and tender affection, the certainty that one or other of them is going to have to go on alone. I think it is particularly important for husbands to ensure that wives know all the necessary details about mortgage, rates, insurance, income tax and so on — where all the necessary papers are — and that there is always a reasonable sum of money in the wife's bank account or in the post office. It may also help the adjustment to retirement to learn a bit about one another's jobs — the maintenance jobs especially, whether of domestic equipment or of clothing, linen and things that women usually look after. There is no reason why this precautionary sharing of skills shouldn't be learned, with jokes and teasing. If one is too squeamish or sentimental or too superstitious to broach the subject, even with the old standby 'I might fall under a bus', there is the serious risk of having a much harder time with the chopped-off remains of one's life than is inevitable.

In our day and age there is no escaping the knowledge that the 'people pattern' includes sexual relations. When young, we all imagine that desire withers with the years as inevitably as the leaves wither on a tree. The gerontologists know — as do all of us who are ageing — that this is not true. Desire can be as fierce in the autumn as in the spring, and can be even more painful, since the odds are so heavily stacked against its being gratified. People write books about it (like *Love and Sex After Sixty*, an American publication by Robert N. Butler and Myrna I. Lewis) to prove that sex is desirable, permissible, enjoyable in the sixties and seventies. But what they do not say and cannot say is how those who have lost their life-time partners, especially women, are to find sexual gratification, however much — after the mourning period is over — they may physically long for it.

This is particularly true for women. The statistic one has to quote over and over again is that there are about 3,000,000 widows to about 800,000 widowers — almost four-to-one odds against finding a second mate. Lonely women who go along to 'lonely hearts' clubs should be warned. Many of us might prefer an affectionate affair to marriage — but is that any more likely? Women in their sixties are often still comely. Grey hair can be charming, or it can be nicely coloured; dieting can keep the figure shapely, make-up can cover up wrinkles and ensure passing for fifty in a subdued light. But so what? To most men the idea of bedding a granny is repulsive. For a man it is different. He is not labelled 'Grandpa' in the way women are labelled 'Granny'. He is admired, if he is well set up, well off and charming to women. A widower is pretty

70

sure of a certain amount of affectionate petting by his female acquaintances, even those much younger than he. But men tend to keep the older widow at a distance, having no wish to be encumbered with an ageing woman who might become clinging or possessive and who would bring no credit to them, as a younger woman would. I think it is true that many women in their sixties, even their seventies, show minimal signs of age, except perhaps for face, hands and feet. Their bosoms are often still soft and shapely, their backs and shoulders smooth, their skin unblemished. But who knows? Who cares?

It seems to me unimaginative, unfeeling and even downright cruel to go on about the desirability of sex to people who may wince in pain from a love passage on the television screen, or find that an old love song brings stinging tears to the eyes. What is much more helpful is to encourage lonely people, women as well as men, to accept the idea of masturbation without embarrassment or disgust. If it gives relief, comfort and sweet sleep, I can see no valid objection to it, though I fully sympathize with the many men and women who think it a poor, shoddy substitute for sexual intercourse with a loving partner. Long-married couples know how to give pleasure to one another, even though they may be either paunchy or scraggy, right into the eighties. Who would not prefer that to a self-induced orgasm?

Our need to give as well as receive affection is often partially met by having a pet. We all know, though, the pathetic extremes this relationship with pets can reach: We have heard how old ladies leave considerable fortunes for the care and maintenance for life of a dog, a cat or even a donkey. I had a childless aunt who kept swallows flying round and messing up her

71

attic and who left a request in her will that her ashes should be buried in her sister's garden, next to the remains of a much loved little cat. (The sister was so outraged by this request that she snorted, 'Never mention it to me again,' and it was left to an unfortunate nephew to collect the ashes from the undertaker. He never revealed how he solved the problem.)

With examples like this, one is wary of seeking the solace of a pet in one's later years. Pets are a tie and a worry if one is often out or away. They are an emotional tie too, and their loss is a harder blow to bear than when one was younger and there were young human beings in the house. All the same, dogs, cats, budgies, parrots, hamsters, guinea pigs have more often saved the sanity of human beings than damaged it. The anti-dog lobby, which has grown so powerful in recent years because of the terrible diseases little children can acquire through contact with canine faeces in parks or gardens, does not take sufficient account of this. On my travels I have learnt that dogs are totally banned in Peking, and also in Reykjavik, the capital of Iceland, so that children will not be afflicted with *Toxicaria canis* or run the risk of rabies and their shoes will not be soiled with evil-smelling excrement.

Mustn't this seem a strange over-reaction though, to millions of people in the cities of the East, where *humans* squat unconcernedly in public places? It is necessary for us to be constantly mindful of hygiene in crowded urban communities; only that way have we conquered the great plagues. The invention of the water-closet was probably the most beneficial of all inventions. But still I feel that *disgust* at excreta, an inevitable part of all animal life, is overdone, psychologically suspect. Matter-of-fact campaigns to keep dogs off the streets and on leads in parks where children play should be sufficient protection.

Let it be said firmly to the 'antis' that a pet is a friend to whom the loneliest person, practically incapable of communication with fellow humans, can talk and express affection. A dog is a spur to go for healthful walks, and a maker of friends, for dog-lovers readily get into conversation with one another. A dog, a cat or other pets, may save the sanity of a bereaved person — often they seem to sense when a display of affection is needed and wag a tail or rub gently against one's legs. There is evidence, on the basis of research done in North America, that owning a pet gives heart-attack patients a better chance of pulling through the first year after a coronary. A professor of psychiatry at Ohio State University found that when he paired fifty elderly unstable patients with dogs, forty-seven of them showed considerable improvement in communication, self-respect and independence.

A group of vets, psychiatrists and doctors formed for the study of the 'human companion-animal bond' believes that the presence of animals in prisons would reduce stress and violence; that they could in certain circumstances be helpful in hospitals; and that among the people who need pets most are those who live alone and alienated in tower blocks — from which, of course, pet animals are firmly banned. It does seem that local authorities and housing associations should take a new look at tenancy clauses which outlaw cats and dogs.

But not all elderly people want the responsibility of an animal friend or even very much like dogs and cats. A friend put into my head a thought which might be helpful to them, however soppy, sentimental or embarrassing it might sound at first. A teddy bear or other soft stuffed toy is quite a useful object to have around the house. You can pick it up and give it a hug as you pass. You can even take it to bed with you and find it is sleep-inducing if clasped to the chest. (Some people use hot water bottles for this purpose, but a bottle that is hot enough to warm a chilly body may be too hot to clasp close to the flesh.) I believe that the number of perfectly rational and capable adults who have teddy bears is quite large, but if the notion seems to risky (what would a son, daughter or other adult visitor think?), there is always the get-out of a pyjama or nightdress case in the form of a basset hound, panda or polar bear. No one need ever know that the pyjama case is Grandpa or Grandma's 'cuddly'. An adult version of the child's 'cuddly' is no more a sign of irrationality or mental disturbance than is masturbation. I say this because of a poignant story told me by a social worker who had had a visit from an elderly widow in serious distress. 'If I tell you something,' said the widow, 'you won't send me to a mental hospital, will you?' It took quite a while for the social worker to convince her that in no circumstances could she or would she send her to a mental home, and that she would not dream of betraying a confidence. But at last the terrible secret came out. Every night since the death of her husband this poor woman had taken a pair of her husband's pyjamas to bed with her. This seemed to her so crazy that she had become convinced she was 'mental' and would be 'put away'.

I told this story at a conference of the National Association of Widows, to illustrate the help that one widow can give to another. 'Any one of you could have helped her, couldn't you?' I asked. There came a heartening chorus of 'Yes'. Pets or no pets, people need people in the later years — much more, perhaps, than those of us who have been surrounded by people all our working lives could ever guess.

4
Preparation

People need to prepare for major changes in their lives — for the first job, marriage, the first home, the first child. We all know that retirement from paid employment is one of the biggest changes in life style that we ever have to make, yet many of us are very reluctant to think about it in advance. Almost every sociologist writing on retirement advises people to start preparing at least ten years before the due date. That means at fifty for a woman, fifty-five for a man. In *Countdown to Retirement* Harry Miller offers a 'count-down' programme — what you do ten years ahead (plan your income because money takes time to accumulate); five years ahead (check on your health in relation to your future activities and decide in principle whether to move or stay put); three years ahead (begin to stockpile semi-durables); two years ahead (decide finally on where to live and get the home decorated throughout); one year ahead (explore job possiblities, including unpaid activities).

An absolutely rational approach — but human beings are not totally rational, and Mr Miller unconsciously touches on the explanation of why so many people are loth to start planning early when he writes: 'The reason for planning in advance is that you bring a younger, fresher mind to the subject. Old age is less

76

flexible, less tolerant and is often unfit to embark on something so complicated as a plan for living. Your plans should be tackled *from strength to weakness'* (my italics). Later Mr Miller adds: 'Life has other peaks than those occasioned by a career. One of the most momentous is attaining the age of 50. Half a century rings a solemn bell. It is at least two-thirds of the way through a working life-time and *retirement begins to cast a shadow'* (my italics again).

From fifty on, one gloomily reflects, it is downhill all the way, in deepening shadow! Isn't this quintessential 'ageism'? The strongest reason for reluctance to prepare for retirement is that in our 'ageist' society it is not an honorable estate. How can one ask a man or woman of fifty-plus, whose family have only recently set up their own establishments, who is still at the peak of his/her career, still ambitious, still working towards the top job in the department or a seat on the board, to divert energy to arrangements for his/her years of 'decline'. Only a few men achieve Cabinet rank before their fifties. The first woman Prime Minister in the Western world is not, surely, to be expected to start preparing for her retirement because she has passed her fiftieth birthday? I am very sure that if anyone had handed me a book on retirement on my fiftieth or even my fifty-fifth birthday, I should have looked at it with as much distaste as if it had been a treatise on sexually transmitted infections.

Thinking back, I feel rather ashamed of what looks now remarkably like sheer cowardice. But during my reading for this book I have come to realize that the reason why we are so unwilling to think out steps towards retirement is that in our society retirement has never been 'institutionalized'. An American sociologist, Clark Tibbits, put it this way: 'Retirement is a relatively new phenomenon in our society and the challenge of a new way of life for most Americans. In rural, pre-industrial days there were comparatively few older adults and most of them were occupied with the responsibility of making a living until over-taken by final illness or death. Partial or complete retirement from work is a development primarily of the last 50 or 75 years.' This is a truth so obvious that it is surprising that it has not been more often stated. 'Coming of age' and marriage have had their powerful rituals in every known society since the dawn of civil-ization, but even in the earlier years of this century there was no retirement procedure — because retire-ment practically did not exist. There is a case for saying that retirement as a way of life in Britain dates only from the introduction of the old age pension in 1911. Clark Tibbits calls retirement 'an outgrowth of the scientific and technological achievements of the time'. It is also a direct result of the formulation of the idea of the Welfare State, which by establishing a pattern of care for those unable to care for themselves has also defined categories of entitlement, of which one is age. It has come about that as you are entitled to receive a pension at the age of sixty (women) or sixty-five (men), it is administratively convenient that you should be *retired* at those ages. You can choose the nature of your first job, you can choose the date of your marriage, but in most cases you have no choice about the date of your retirement. And what you make of it is entirely up to you.

As another American, Wayne E. Thompson, puts it, 'The retiree must create for himself a pattern of activities which serves as an effective substitute for his job. Thus adjustment in retirement involves a personal input over and above that required to assimilate new activities and patterns of interaction which stand ready-made and waiting as part of a well-defined institutional structure.'

So there are two potentially alarming thoughts about the approach of the Day of Departure — one that it will be a step into the unknown and unpredictable, the other that it will almost inevitably bring a substantial loss of income, a probable loss of status and a possible loss of contacts. Generally speaking, the more disagreeable or stressful the job and the lower the pay, the more one is ready to leave it. The higher one's status in employment, the greater the reluctance to give up. But only you yourself can bring yourself up to the starting-post. At some point, unless you are in the sort of employment where everyone knows your age as well as your grade, you have to let people know — not your employer; he knows all right — that you are due to go. It may feel like announcing an impending bankruptcy, and if so, the only advice one can give is to choose a suitable colleague, invite him or her out to lunch, get a few drinks under your belt if you feel you need to and then say 'Did you know that I am due to retire on . . .?' The relief of having 'made confession' is enormous. The word will soon spread round, and you yourself will begin to comprehend that being no longer in full-time paid employment is not demeaning, pathetic or somehow disgraceful. Long years ago a woman said to a suffrage worker, 'Being a spinster must be very nice once you have got over the disgrace.' Being a retired person can also be quite delectable once you have coped with your hang-ups.

The hang-ups are due, of course, to the images of old age which are discussed elsewhere in this book, and I hope it may become clear to people now in advanced middle age that there is a lot of work to be done in making 'senior citizenhood' not a trite euphemism for 'redundancy' but a prestigious state that they might aspire to rather than dread. It is in this sort of way, that bodies like the Pre-Retirement Association can help most, helping 'retirees' to see themselves as comrades-in-arms.

The Pre-Retirement Association was set up in 1964 to encourage retirement training and to run courses. It has only about 1,000 individual members, but it has extended its influence widely and powerfully among big firms and corporations such as Barclay's and the Midland bank, the British Steel Corporation, Bovis and Curry's. It has a lively magazine, *Choice,* which has a monthly circulation of at least 80,000, much of it through firms' bulk orders. The Pre-Retirement Association places strong emphasis on the duty of employers to encourage retirement training and the maintenance of links between former and present staff. *Choice* quotes the trade-union leader Jack Jones as saying, 'I honestly believe that pre-retirement training should now become part of our collective bargaining in industry. So far as I personally have influence in negotiations, we want to do more in that direction.'

Consultations, counselling, study courses and seminars, kits and conferences — the Pre-Retirement Association covers the field thoroughly, with an emphasis on persuading firms to do their duty by long-service employees but also with an eye to individuals. The former director and general secretary of the association, Fred Kemp and Bernard Buttle, collaborated on a book entitled *Focus on Retirement.* The present director, William Bruce, concentrates on a personal approach and will talk at conferences at every level, of shop-floor workers, clergy and other professional men right up to gatherings of the topmost brass, where the participants may be earning £20,000 to £30,000 a year. Bill Bruce has a nice brisk attitude to his job — perhaps because he views it from a long previous experience in industry. In 1951 he started training textile workers and says he reduced the training time for weavers from eighteen months to ten weeks, mainly by the use of the written word in easily assimilated form. 'They learned bit by bit,' he claims, 'The same with the foremen. We didn't give them a manual and frighten them to death. The foremen built up their own training manual.'

Bill Bruce thinks the same methods should be extended to retirement planning. 'A little often is better than a lot at once.' His kits include recommended books, pamphlets and notes giving guidance on various aspects of retirement planning, such as mental attitudes, health, money, a future home, employment and voluntary work and other leisure interests, and both individuals and companies can order them.

Bill Bruce's job is virtually 'selling' retirement preparation, and he says frankly that his problems come 'at the top end and at the bottom end'.

In the factory or any large company, if retirement preparation is not sold properly and adequately, it will be received badly, misinterpreted and treated with suspicion because people will think it looks as if the skids are under them. But it can be a realistic effort to assist employees to get the most out of almost as many years of life in the future as they have had actually working for the firm. The idea is that there is a lot of joy awaiting them — I know that sounds high-falutin', but it's true. We have to sell the idea through the unions, on the shop floor, as well as through management, so that it is not seen as a way of getting rid of old Joe without trouble, but as a means of helping him to enjoy what he has earned . . .. The 'retiree' should become a member of the 'old-timers club' or whatever it is called *before* retirement so that he starts re-educating himself in ample time.

The difficulty at the other end of the money scale is exactly the opposite of 'maintaining motivation'. It is, so to speak, reducing the voltage of the current that drives on the men whom Bill Bruce calls 'the Top Brass'. These men have immense commitments. They run vast enterprises. There are millions of pounds at stake and they are responsible for the existence of thousands of people. They are what we call 'workaholics', and they naturally think, 'I am indispensable to my firm and I have got much more important things to think about than retirement.'

There is something these men (and there are some women too in this category now) have forgotten: that in the articles of association of their supra-national companies there is a provision that managing directors and chairmen retire at 65. Such people have no reason to worry much about money. What hits them like a thunderbolt is that, come the day, they will have nothing, but NOTHING to do.

It is probably more important for 'top people' than for anyone to face the fact of retirement in good time. They have the chance of arranging a part-time seat on the board, a consultancy or a useful job on a Quango, a Government or industrial consultative body, perhaps even of running a National Trust property or a nature reserve. Top people have contacts and influence. It would be foolish if they failed to take soundings in good time.

Fred Kemp and Bernard Buttle relate in their book one of the success stories of industrial pre-retirement planning — by the Ford Motor Company, which started a scheme in the early 1960s when it had fewer than 1,000 pensioners. Now it has 11,000. In the Pre-Retirement Association's magazine *Choice* Del Pasterfield, supervisor of welfare programmes, wrote, 'Many pensioners were writing to us about matters unconnected with pensions and some for no apparent reason at all. Many problems of loneliness, ill-adjustment and ill-health came to our notice.' This led to the establishment of the 'Ford Pensioners' Association'. Twelve hand-picked pensioners were selected as visitors to launch a pilot scheme in the Essex area. Each visitor was provided with a list of pensioners in his location and sufficient stationery to organize his visiting. Out-of-pocket expenses were paid. The scheme now has 150 visitors, reaching out to pensioners all over Britain. 'They meet with us at our annual conference to discuss Ford news, results and ideas for future progress. There is also a Ford news letter.'

Messrs Kemp and Buttle also tell of the Action for Independent Maturity organization in the USA set up by the American Association of Retired Persons, which claims to be 'the largest and most active organization in the world for helping retired people to pack the greatest enjoyment into their lives', with a membership of 7,000,000 and a vociferous lobby in Washington. The membership of Action for Independent

Maturity is open to people of fifty to sixty-five, who get a bi-monthly magazine called *Dynamic Maturity*. It was from this powerful organization that the truly dynamic pressure group, the Grey Panthers, sprang.

'Dynamic maturity' may not exactly describe what many of us have in mind for our retirement. 'Positive value orientation', a popular phrase with American sociologists, is not a comfortable concept either. It is better, perhaps, to talk now in rather more down-to-earth terms of what one can do, off one's own bat, to prepare. Obviously, after psychological preparation the most important planning is financial. Specialist help is available from many sources. One's own bank manager and accountant can give sound advice about investments and tax claims. Local Citizens' Advice Bureaux, branches of Age Concern and local authority welfare departments readily supply information about the benefits available to pensioners. If you don't ask, you don't find out. It may be slightly embarrassing to apply for one's first Senior Citizen rail card, or one's first concessionary bus pass or coupons, and to wave one's pension book at the doorkeeper of a musuem or stately home is a disconcerting reminder of one's reduced financial status. But the facilities are there for us, like free prescriptions, chiropody services, lower subscriptions, fees and so on. There is no reason why one should not patronize a hairdresser who gives cut-price rates to pensioners on Mondays — or a fish and chip shop which gives 30p off on certain days! — any more than one should hesitate to book on cut-price winter holidays. I have yet to hear of anyone who refuses the income tax relief for the over-sixty-fives. (Indeed, most women on pensions are indignant that they do not get the 'age relief' between sixty and sixty-five.)

Harry Miller's 'countdown' plan touches on one aspect of retirement preparation which is important partly because it is enjoyable as well as commonsense in inflationary days — stock-piling. Alas, in these days money saved tends to lose value rapidly, but 'durables' do not. (They can, like very good china, unused and carefully stored, even be an investment.) Of course, the best investment for one's old age is a suitable home, suitably furnished and suitably equipped. Expenditure to make the home as you have always wanted it can be a real joy in the years after the children are truly independent and your income is at its peak. That is not to say that one should sacrifice present enjoyment to future comfort; it is just a reminder that a few hundreds spent now on installing central heating will be a first-class investment — even in the financial sense of being able to sell your house much more profitably if ever you decide to leave. Keeping warm effortlessly is a priceless boon in one's later years. While you are at it, you might as well investigate the possibilities of double-glazing, roof insulation, draught exclusion and so forth.

Is your bathroom to your liking? Wouldn't a heated bath-rail be a delicious luxury? Or a wall electric fire? Why not re-do the whole bathroom in a style and colour to your fancy? And, while you are at it, have handles fixed to the sides of the bath — stiff knees are especially a nuisance when it comes to hoisting yourself out of the bath. Curtains and carpets are now extremely expensive and will probably become more so in relation to your retirement income. Why not go into the 'days of choice' with a bit of panache? A formica-topped dining-table is fashionable and looks very well with table mats. Linen tablecloths are handsome but costly to send to the laundry and a considerable labour to wash and iron at home.

When sons and daughters and generous friends and relations ask for suggestions about Christmas and birthday presents, steer them, if you can, away from purely ornamental objects of any kind and suggest they might perhaps club together for useful equipment. A continental duvet means not only that you will never again have to pull up, straighten and tuck in sheets and blankets but also that you will be snugly warm, without either electric blanket or hot water bottle, for most of the year. Modern kitchen equipment is most welcome, too — one of the new mixer-mincer-liquidizer jobs, or a slow electric cooking pot. Fathers may appreciate an electric drill, a lightweight lawn-mower or a small greenhouse. Hobbies can be encouraged — an electric sewing machine, a portable typewriter, an elegant filing cabinet, the latest in stereo reproduction.

Odd though it may sound, stock-piling good clothes can be sensible, too. The thought came to me when I realized that a cashmere twin-set bought seventeen years ago was still perfectly wearable. Why not a similar cashmere cardigan, while I can easily afford it, which will carry me cosily and smartly into my great old age if need be? And a fur (or fur-fabric) coat? And why not, for a man, a really good, well-cut tweed jacket, which will never either 'date' or look unpleasantly shabby? Expensive clothes, no doubt of it, do boost one's ego. A friend who was on her uppers for several years kept up her spirits and her professional image by hanging on, come what may, to a rather dramatic full-length fox-fur coat. It saw her through until brains and luck combined to put her back in the money.

Medical check-ups are an obvious aspect of preparation for retirement, but how much thought to take about future health problems is a matter of temperament as well as of past experience. A man who knows he suffers from high blood pressure and therefore risks a stroke or cerebral spasm will obviously take precautions, as far as he can, to avoid stress, as well as to cut down on smoking, drinking and rich eating. But whether he gets in touch with the Chest, Heart and Stroke Association to find out what help is available in case he does have a crippling stroke depends entirely on the kind of person he is. Some people are much calmer and more courageous if they are well prepared for the worst that may befall. Others can fret themselves into a low state or into actual ill-health just by reading about all the disabilities elderly people may be subject to — failing sight, failing hearing, failing bladder control, failing mobility and so on. There are people who should not be allowed within a mile of a medical dictionary or even a 'health in old age' booklet.

This is where a good partner is an invaluable asset, of course, to coax the recalcitrant spouse into making regular visits to the doctor, the oculist and the chriopodist; to encourage him or her to accept that a hearing aid will make conversation (and attendance at meetings, etc.) much more enjoyable; to investigate the local possibilities of fitness classes specially geared to maintaining and increasing health in later years. At the best of these 'exercise' classes people are taught to take their own pulse, so the danger of overdoing it is ruled out. Advice on preparing for retirement is apt to sound unrealistic, patronizing or sentimental, but there is one piece of advice everyone in his/her sixties and seventies would endorse — keep mobile. If you give up golf or squash in your later middle years, take up bowls; if you give up jogging, arrange to walk part of the way to work; take up old-tyme dancing if you have a taste for it, or yoga, or any kind of 'keep fit' programme; or discipline yourself into doing a few minutes' bending and stretching exercises in the bathroom every day. You can't expect to be able to relax muscles that have been stiffening for years immediately you decide, in your sixties, to go to a class; and you may well find, if you have let yourself grow stiff in the joints, that the one thing that makes you really 'feel your age' is the sight of a young man or woman running, with powerful and easy grace, for the bus that you have resigned yourself to missing.

5
Pleasures

People of any age need something to do. Only men and women of exceptional will power and intellect can survive enforced idleness, as in solitary confinement. Faculties, whether mental or physical, which are not used tend to atrophy. Many of the casualties of retirement are the people who, for one reason or another, give up. It is important to give quite a lot of thought to what we are going to *do* when we finish with paid employment. The common idea that retirement is a reward for a life of hard and incessant toil and that we are all going to enjoy endless, lovely stress-free days is dangerous nonsense. Leisure is precious when it is a contrast to work, just as being alone is a delightful change from being surrounded by too many people claiming our attention.

There are two vitally important things to remember: one that for the first time in your life you can choose how you spend your time, subject only to the limits of your strength and your purse, and both can be stretched further than you may imagine. The second is that pastimes that just 'put the time on' in the old north country phrase, are not really much use. One needs pursuits that will give continuing fulfilment. Are you thinking of weeding and mowing the garden? Weeds do not grow in winter. Neither does the grass.

Are you thinking of tiling the bathroom and kitchen? Once it is done it is done. One patchwork quilt will probably be enough, even if you have a clutch of hopeful granddaughters. A hobby that does not grow and develop can easily become a bore. Have you heard the story of the little boy who when asked what he was doing said 'It's me 'obby and I 'ate it'?

Dr Alex Comfort, the gerontologist who has given us better, funnier and more often quoted stories about ageing than anyone, told me of a man he met when he was flying the Atlantic to attend the launch of his incomparable book *A Good Age.* This man was grumbling about having to travel so much and said he was determined to retire at sixty-two. 'And what are you going to do then?' asked Dr Comfort. 'Fish', said the man. 'Are you going to be a professional fisherman then?' 'Oh no. I just want to go and catch salmon.' So Dr Comfort told him, 'You can do that for about two months and then you will have caught so many salmon that you'll never want to see another for the rest of your life.' Not only the little children for whom Robert Louis Stevenson wrote his *A Child's Garden of Verses* but people who have been too busy for years to stop and look around them should heed his words:

> The world is so full of a number of things
> I'm sure we should all be as happy as kings.

Which of all these 'numbers of things' is for you? Only you know. One of the most aggravating myths about the elderly is that they are a well-defined category with the same wants, needs, interests and abilities. They are no more a category than teenagers or forty-year-olds. We come into the world totally different from one another and different we remain to the end. I suppose I should even amend my positive assertion that *everyone* needs a regular occupation. Some rare souls, like contemplatives, can just sit and think and ponder the mysteries of life. Equally there are rare people who have an insatiable desire to go and see. I heard of one man who when he was well past eighty would suddenly decide to get out his car and drive to see the Boston Stump or the Severn Bore, just because he never had.

Though the pastime that was just a pleasant time-filler after work will not develop into an important part of one's later life, some of the things we do for fun can be even more rewarding in one's later years when there is more time to give to them. Talking about the pleasures of life I will start with my own — not because my hobbies are the best hobbies, but because I hope the pleasure I get from them will be infectious and persuade other people to enjoy life, in this way or that. My own best 'hobby', no question, is singing. I can't remember when I started. Certainly I sang for my grandmother when I was very little; I was praised for singing the morning hymn nicely at school when I was about six; I used to sit at the piano, accompanying myself very badly hoping that passers-by would hear me and admire, in my early teens; I sang always in school choirs (alto, because I could hold the part) and in my first 'ladies choir' at seventeen. Later I sang in choirs as famous as the Hallé Chorus and as exciting as the Cantata Choir at Manchester Cathedral. When I was about sixty my voice began to disintegrate into a croak. I could scarcely even sing nursery rhymes for my granddaughter. I raged and grieved and cursed old age — but it was my addiction to nicotine that was the chief trouble. In my mid-sixties I went down with pneumonia and was solemnly warned against smoking by doctor and chest consultant. It appeared to me as my one chance to get rid of a dirty, expensive and dangerous habit. I couldn't, surely, feel much worse, through withdrawal symptoms, than I already did? I did feel worse. I still miss the stimulus of a cigarette when I start writing and the comfort of a cigarette after a meal. But within two years I found I could sing again, and nothing, nothing, will now persuade me to risk losing that supreme pleasure. (By one of the happy coincidences, which surely are as frequent as the unhappy ones, my chest consultant also sings alto in the very choir in which I currently sing.)

Of course, at seventy your voice isn't as it was at seventeen; you have to watch a tendency to go flat when you are straining for upper notes; you'll never sing a solo lead again. On the other hand, after all those years you can read quite difficult music with comparative ease and may be a reassurance to some of your fellows who rely on you to come in bang on the note, dead on the beat! There is something exquisitely satisfying to the whole man (or woman), to body, mind and spirit in singing — especially the fellowship, the being part of a communal experience. Even people who only join in pub sing-songs or old-time choruses at pensioners' socials know that. Did some sarcastic schoolmaster tell you it would be as well if you shut up, as one told my music-loving husband in his teens? Forget him: he had a hang-over or his corns hurt him. Did you never learn to read music? You aren't alone in that — a high proportion of choir singers, especially sopranos, learn by ear. (Conductors quite like them, because once they have learned the notes, by mimicry, they take their noses out of the score!) There are Women's Institute choirs, Townswomen's Guild choirs, lots and lots of church and local authority choirs which welcome recruits and don't have auditions. Many years ago I read in the then *Manchester Guardian* of an octogenarian who had taken part in Evensong at the church in which he had been a chorister for most of his life, went into the vestry, and there died of a heart attack. I wish I thought my own end would be like that.

In the reigns of Good Queen Bess, King James and King Charles it was not only respectable for a man to read music and sing it but almost as necessary as being able to read words. To reassure men who have never ventured further than singing in the bath or at an old school reunion — Prince Charles sings. He told me so himself when I was presented to him at a function and rather impertinently asked him if he still played the cello. 'No,' he said, 'I haven't time. But I sing.' ('Oh, sir,' I couldn't resist saying, 'so do I!')

Prince Charles paints, too, as did Sir Winston Churchill and many other distinguished people. They must have encouraged quite a lot of high-powered executives, quite remote from the world of local education authority and Workers' Educational Association classes, to 'have a go'. Painting is almost as pure a pleasure as singing — not *quite* as pure, I think, because apart from the people who enter for music festivals, there is usually no competitive element in singing, whereas for painters there are classes, tutorials, exhibitions and painting holidays where the work is assessed and some paintings are chosen and others not.

Speaking as one who has never had a painting chosen for exhibition and is not likely to, I can say, hand on heart, that that has never spoilt the pleasure for me. On my sitting-room walls are paintings (not necessarily my best) of the Great Wall of China, the Parthenon of Athens, a château in the Dordogne, an archway in Rhodes, a doorway in a hill village in Spain, a loch in the Mull of Kintyre, a small harbour in Malta, a snow cloud in the Tyrol. As I look at them, my heart swells with pleasure and joy. I take holiday photographs, too, and give a lot of thought to the time, the place and the angle, but the veriest daub is better, I think, for recalling the *feeling* I had about the place.

Paintings don't, of course, have to be of places. They can be of pots and pans, people, plants or ideas and perceptions. One of the most exciting painting stories is that of my very old friend Gertrude Boyd, born in 1884. When she was ninety-four the friend with whom she shares a flat took an Open University course on the history of art. Gertrude read the books and her friend's essays — and that started her off. The natural starting-point was greetings cards, because Gertrude, who has an immense circle of friends, had for years made her own, all to one design, with exquisite lettering. These new cards were different. In thick poster or acrylic paint, on brightly coloured stiff paper, she let her brush make twirls and swirls, arcs and lines and blodges. Everyone was different, everyone a flash of inspiration. She showed her first batch to friends and acquaintances, taking a collection for her favourite good cause, the National Society for the Prevention of Cruelty to Children. Then she took to painting larger and more ambitious designs, and the weekend after her ninety-fifth birthday had a two-day party, to receive congratulations and give her paintings to any friends who fancied them.

Gertrude says (and it is obvious from the ebullience of her colours and shapes), 'I've got a terrific feeling

94

about my painting. It takes the place of writing letters to friends. Most days I can't write with the pen; my hand shakes too much. But that doesn't stop me using the brush. The shaky hand can even be an advantage, because it produces a graceful, wavering line instead of a hard, straight one.' Some of her most original cards were painted in the middle of the night, when she couldn't sleep.

Shaky hands, arthritic hands, even paralysed hands will not stop anyone who has a powerful urge to paint. Some of the Mouth and Foot painters, like Elizabeth Twistington-Higgins, who specializes in studies of dancers, do very good work. Most people know that 'Grandma Moses', the world-famous American 'primitive' painter, was quite an old woman when she started painting. It is less widely known that she started painting because she found, when she was seventy-eight, that her fingers were too stiff to hold an embroidery needle any longer. Anna Mary Moses painted on until she died at the age of 101; her paintings gave great pleasure and fetched very high prices right round the world.

It is true that if a thing is worth doing, it is worth doing well, and that pleasure is greater if one takes trouble to learn technique. But I think a thing is also worth doing if, by professional standards, it is done 'badly' — if it is done with feeling, with commitment and emotional release. I have been on many painting holidays, and I am by no means sure that the people who got the most out of them were the most accomplished painters. Mercifully, when we look at our darling paintings we see — at least in the first flush of creation — what we want to see, and it doesn't matter all that much that other people are aware of our deficiencies.

You have to be a bit more realistic about your products when it comes to gardening. A slug-bitten radish is a slug-bitten radish, however miraculous it may seem to you that you have grown it at all. But we can go on gardening after a fashion until our very late years and get mental as well as physical health out of it. It was just after her ninety-fifth birthday that I asked Dame Margery Corbett Ashby whether she was still able to work in her beautiful Sussex garden. 'Oh, yes,' she said, 'I can weed on hands and knees.' 'But how do you get up again?' I asked, being afflicted with obstinately stiff knees myself. 'Oh, I put one hand on my fork and one on my trug and push myself up,' she said. She added, in a confidential tone of voice, that what she was really good at was *sawing*. At ninety-seven she was still weeding her garden on hands and knees, with a whistle round her neck to summon help to get back on to her feet!

Gnarled, a little bent, skin as brown and wrinkled as a walnut, gardeners seem to go on as long as painters (Michelangelo, Picasso), musicians (Sir Adrian Boult, Rubinstein) and philosophers (Bertrand Russell, Geroge Bernard Shaw). One recalls affectionately the heart-warming 'Cheerio' of Radio 4's Saturday gardener, Fred Streeter, broadcast only a few hours before he died at the age of eighty-eight. Contact with the earth seems particularly energizing and the best cure ever known for depression, ill-temper, boredom — even loneliness. Now and again a cat will sit on the wall and keep you company, the birds will certainly chirrup and a robin may perch on your spade handle if you turn your back for long. I first read Rudyard Kipling's poem 'The Camel's Hump' when I was a little girl, but it has stayed with me all my life:

The cure for this ill is not to sit still,
And frowst with a book by the fire;
But to take a large hoe and a shovel also,
And dig till you gently perspire.

And then you will find that the sun and the wind,
And the Djinn of the Garden too,
  Have lifted the hump —
  The horrible hump —
The hump that is black and blue!

No hobby has better tangible rewards. To eat the beans, potatoes, carrots, cabbage or cauliflowers one has grown is an immense satisfaction. So is the cutting and arranging of a mixed bunch of flowers. To achieve flower arrangements as lovely and as varied with shop-bought flowers would cost a great deal of money and be far less enjoyable. There is another thing: being close to nature in this way makes one (to use a phrase of John Masefield's) 'less certain of the fearful grave'. In the garden everything 'dies' and everything lives again, if not in the same form, at least in humus that enriches the soil. There will always be another spring; the crocuses will always pierce through iron-hard, snow-covered soil; the apple trees and the raspberries will fruit again, even if we are not here to see them. It seemed to me a splendid affirmation when a seventy-seven-year-old friend, newly established in a 'sheltered' flat development, planted six tomato plants in the small strip of earth under his sitting-room window. No bought tomatoes would ever taste as good as his. He counted every one, up to a total of seventy-two!

If the labour of digging and hoeing and even weeding becomes too heavy, there is always kitchen-window gardening. (Though it is astonishing what even creaky old limbs can manage. I once planted out five new roses with a broken right arm.) Given the right compost and the right care, almost any seed or pip will put up a shoot and send down a root. Stick an avocado stone in a narrow jar of water and, if you are lucky as well as patient, you may see one morning that the little point at the base of the stone has pushed through. In time it will be a firm, branched root; the brown skin will peel off, and the creamy white 'flesh' will split apart to allow a purplish stalk to thrust up from the centre which, in time, will bear lustrous leaves and may grow as much as two feet tall. I don't know anyone who has actually grown an edible avocado indoors, but I do have a friend who has grown green peppers (capsicums) from seed scraped from a red pepper bought at the greengrocer's. My dream is now to grow an aubergine, since I discovered, in the garden of a convent perched on the top of a mountain in north-west Greece, why the aubergine's other name is 'egg plant'. There, lying on the sun-baked earth, were glossy, creamy-white 'eggs'. It wasn't until one of us bobbed down and saw that one 'egg' was colouring purple that we added this new fact to our gardening lore. From two little dried-up twigs of basil brought home illicitly from the Greece holiday seedlings are at this moment poking through the compost. One can do all sorts of things in the 'kitchen' garden. I once had two morning glory plants climbing up the cord of an old Venetian blind above my sink. Alas, they turned their backs on me, and I had to run into the front garden to appreciate the full beauty of their glorious blue.

Other people's hobbies are just as absorbing and enlivening to them as mine are to me. One friend drives twice a week from a Norfolk village to her bridge club in Norwich and wins cups and other awards; another, who has for years woven anything from ties and belts to cushion covers and even lengths of material adequate to cover a granddaughter's sofa, has now taken to spinning as well and knits for her daughters and *their* daughters charming caps from natural shades of brown, grey, beige and cream wool which she has spun herself.

Another friend took an Open University course in medieval history; another went to a Workers' Educational Association class in historical documents and archives. The variety of classes and courses offered by the Workers' Educational Association, university extra-mural department, local education authorities and others always astounds me. Here is a very small selection, indicating the immense range, from the classes beginning with 'R' offered by the Inner London Education Authority in its brochure *Floodlight.* There is, of course 'Retirement' (nine classes in various areas) and, in addition, there are thirteen courses on 'cookery in retirement' and twenty on 'keeping fit in retirement'. Some other 'Rs': radio maintenance, repair and servicing, radio techniques, railways, rambling, rating and valuation, reading and writing, refrigeration technology, relaxation, religions, report writing, restoration (of books, furniture, documents or ceramics), retailing, road-traffic engineering, rock music, roller skating, Romance linguistics, Romanian and Russian language at all levels and for all purposes. Provincial cities may not have quite the range of classes offered by Inner London, but the choice will be wide, and local education authorities and Workers' Educational Associations are always responsive to demand. Collect a group of a dozen or even fewer, wanting to study anything from nuclear physics to naval architecture, and great efforts will be made to secure a qualified tutor.

You don't, of course, have to attend a class to enjoy discussions and participate in interesting pursuits. In most areas you can find poetry or play-reading groups as well as drama societies — and if you are too self-conscious in your later years to act, there are always plenty of behind the scenes jobs for both men and women, from costume-making to prompting and stage lighting. Many elderly people have told me that what they miss most is intelligent conversation. I came upon an admirable and quite aged lady who had monthly gatherings in her home and insisted that the participants should listen to radio plays and talks, go to exhibitions or theatres and bring ideas to discuss at each meeting. This may be difficult as we grow really old and less able to get about, but the tape recorder has opened up new possibilities of communication. There is always likely to be some mobile friend who will collect and deliver cassettes which can provide stimulating thoughts for 'answer tapes'. How do you get in touch with like-minded people? The notice board of the local public lending library is probably the best way. Local newspapers and local radio stations are almost invariably helpful.

Collecting is a continuing pleasure for many people and often provides an incentive to get out and about. Teapots, glasses, matchbox covers, buttons, coins, bottles, medals — the knowledgeable pursuit is the pleasure, though the displaying of the treasures is also a pleasure and can be shared very happily by an artistic partner. Laying the foundations of a wine cellar is a rather similar satisfaction, since it needs study of vintages and vineyards as well as a watchful eye for bargains — and it has the additional value that it will encourage valued old friends to pay a visit!

I confess to itchy feet. One of the greatest pleasures of later years is the greater possibility of travel — at times when all the world and his wife and family are not also on the move. A woman friend who retired thankfully from her heavy social services job as soon as she could takes on various jobs in her field, lasting a few weeks or even a few months, with the sole aim of earning enough money to travel. In the last few years she has travelled, literally, from China to Peru and to many places on both sides of the Iron Curtain, not to write about them or to take slides to show to her friends but because she has an insatiable curiosity about 'foreign parts'. She even sold her garden for a large sum and said smugly, 'That's two more good trips abroad.' She has acquired some interesting, beautiful and exciting souvenirs on her travels, which somehow settle down harmoniously in her elegant flat, despite their different cultural origins, but most importantly she is stocking her mind with experiences which will prevent her in her late years from ever being a bore to herself or anyone else.

I myself spent my seventy-first birthday — most unexpectedly, because of a legacy from an aunt — in a commune of Gong-Xian country north-west China. That sixteen-day trip to China opened up a vast new area of interest to me — not only the antiquities, the paintings, the language and its calligraphy and the staggering inventiveness of this remarkable people of whom I had previously known so little, but the whole political scene of the Far East. To have been in Peking even as an ordinary tourist, at a time when China was changing course after the death of Chairman Mao and the fall of the Gang of Four was to feel an involvement with China's future and thereafter to follow eagerly news of China in the newspapers and periodicals, on radio and television. I have no doubt at all that I invested my aunt's legacy admirably.

One of the most important things about holidays is that they are something to look forward to, something on the other side of the hill, round the next bend in the road, or however you like to put it. The importance of holidays for the ageing as well as for children is, in fact, coming to be much more widely appreciated. A number of local authorities, like the borough of Camden, for instance, provide through their social services department two weeks' holiday for pensioners, or, alternatively, assistance with fares.

Many travel firms provide out-of-season bargains for the elderly, and Saga, a company based in Folkestone, has made this big business (obviously profitable) by offering remarkable holiday bargains in Portugal, Spain, Yugoslavia and Britain. With three friends I once spent the whole month of February in the Algarve, in a villa which is part of a tourist village, Aldeia Turistica, largely built by the Saga company. We could scarcely credit how reasonable our bungalow was, with the service of two cheerful local ladies who came in to wash up, make beds and tidy up. We watched the almond blossom flourish and fade and the mimosa come into bloom; we sat in a sheltered corner of the beach and watched the little waves roll in; we took the local train to Faro, where the main square was lined with orange trees in full fruit and there was a stork's nest on a church tower, and to Lagos, where there is a church which seems to be lined with pure gold. We made our way to the hill village of Alte, where the political slogans painted in red on every wall were particularly lively (one we translated as 'Down with the hammer and sickle; up with Black and Decker'). When we walked along the cliffs to the little town of Albufeira to buy vegetables or fish for lunch, two friendly dogs usually accompanied us. There were always visiting grey tabby cats, looking so much alike that when my companions decided that I could entertain and feed just one of them, they tied a piece of blue wool round her neck and said to her sternly, 'Don't lose it. That's your meal ticket!'

We shall never forget the prickly pear hedges, the huge carafes of cheap red wine we carried down from the little village self-service store. But most of all we shall remember the wonderful sense of freedom. All working women, we had always had to ration our holidays to a fortnight. Here we were, with a whole month of free time, in beautiful scenery in a beautiful climate. There were scores of equally happy pensioners in other villas and apartments and in the specially built Aldeia Turistica hotel. I am prepared to bet that quite a few people who have never felt they could afford a holiday abroad in all their working lives have gone on Saga and similar holidays. You see them at railway stations and airports, looking a little nervous, with their bright yellow badges — and you may see them on their return, bronzed, happy and confident that there is another trip abroad to look forward to next year.

Those of us who regard holidays as a sort of fuel for living find it difficult to appreciate that there are many thousands of retired people who never have a holiday away from home at all. Saving up for it is the ostensible difficulty, but simply not knowing what the possibilities of subsidized holidays are is even worse. Mrs Betty Hunter, the director of a small

103

charity, The National Benevolent Fund for the Aged, became interested in the possibility of helping people to have holidays while she was working with the Chest, Heart and Stroke Association, and since she set up a holidays for the elderly scheme in 1961, she has arranged trips for 11,500 pensioners from all over Britain. The holiday centres are in Ilfracombe, Morecambe and Llandudno, all for healthy and active guests who have been recommended by health visitors, district nurses and so on. They travel by coach to and from the resort and enjoy free accommodation at the hotel and free entertainment, which costs the National Benevolent Fund for the Aged at least £40 a head. Raising the money, as well as organizing the accommodation and travel, is Mrs Hunter's job. Legacies have been a very substantial help – indeed, it was a large bequest in 1970 that started off the holiday scheme and the organizing of Christmas outings for frail old people and the provision of television sets for housebound people living alone.

Since 1979 holidays for 350 frail and physically handicapped people have been planned at a hotel in Rothbury, Northumberland. Couriers have to be found for all the holidays, but for the frail and disabled extra care is obviously needed. Holidays for the elderly, whether at home or abroad, are not a burden on the hotel and travel industries – quite the reverse. Of Ilfracombe, perhaps her favourite resort, Mrs Hunter said, 'All the hotels love it, because it extends their season by a fortnight.' And the visitors love it because in the spring and autumn resorts are less crowded; shop-keepers often reduce their prices; and the hotels put on a tremendous effort to please their elderly guests, who, of course, are apt to be far more appreciative than other visitors. After all, one of the criteria for enjoying a trip organized by the National Benevolent Fund for the Aged is that one has not had a holiday for five years or more.

Not everyone wants to travel to China as I did, to Calais by Hovercraft, or even to Morecambe or Ilfracombe with a party. Catching a bus to the nearest Age Concern 'pop-in-parlour', walking to a day centre, taking a midday meal at a senior citizens' luncheon club at least keeps one on one's feet and provides company. But more taxing physical exercise is marvellous fun for those who have kept fit and supple all their lives. Many people enjoy physical exercise into their eighties, even in forms that younger people find exhausting. I haven't ridden a bicycle for years, but my father cycled to his work until his death at the age of sixty-nine (and he also kept a large allotment garden well cultivated and productive). Journalists in Manchester have been brought up on the story of C. P. Scott, the world-famous editor of the *Manchester Guardian,* who was addressed by a policeman as he rode home late at night from the office in Cross Street, in the centre of the city, to Victoria Park, more than a mile away. 'What are you doing out at this time of night?' the kindly bobby asked the white-bearded old gentleman. 'Cycling home from work,' replied C.P. 'Well, I think it's a shame they should keep a poor old bugger like you out until this hour,' said the constable. As petrol shortages grow worse, more people will take to cycles; why not the newly retired, just as much as the young? Our incomes are less able to cope with car maintenance and the rising cost of petrol, and our need to travel long distances tends to shrink. The thing about cycling is that you never forget *how* and never lose the basic sense of balance. You do tend though to lose confidence and the speed of physical reaction, so it is not very wise to exchange the car for a couple of bicycles the day you retire.

Many local authorities organize swimming and bowls for the elderly, and there are also plenty of keep-fit classes which welcome people with tummy bulges and stiff joints. The Employment Fellowship now has under its umbrella an organization named Extend, which trains nurses, paramedicals and League of Health and Beauty teachers in methods of physical exercise suitable for elderly and disabled people. It has had some notable successes in helping retired men and women to overcome their disabilities. A woman of seventy-seven who had had a quite severe stroke learned to walk without her stick and get herself up-stairs to her bed instead of sleeping on a sofa in her sitting-room. An eighty-four-year-old woman had to be heaved out of her daughter's car when she first came to her class. At the class she loosened up her joints and so strengthened her feeble leg muscles that she was soon able to do her daughter's shopping as well as her own. She told everyone that she attended 'youth and beauty' classes. An elderly man, on the other hand, told his friends that he attended a 'health and vigour' class, and his arthritis was so much relieved that he won a 'walking for health' competition.

The mental muscles can grow flabby as well as the physical ones in later years, especially if the challenges at work lessen. There is nothing like a bout of ener-getic campaigning to firm them up. Have no diffi-dence about offering your help to any campaign that raises your adrenalin. Now that you have that most precious commodity, time, you will seem to the cam-paigners a pearl beyond price. You will find that the 'US against THEM' syndrome is an incomparable youth-restorer, especially as you are likely to be working with many much younger people. We all have our own adrenalin-raisers — pavement parking, juggernaut lorries, litter, vandalism, public spending cuts that threaten the closure of small hospitals and homes for the aged, kerb-crawling, mugging — there is sure to be the nucleus of a campaigning group locally, whose activities are reported in the local newspaper or can be traced through the local library or the Citizens Advice Bureau.

It seems to me sad that the 'Reclaim the Night' campaign is left to quite young women some of whom, through over-enthusiasm perhaps, have come into conflict with the police. I truly believe that every citizen has an equal right to walk the streets safely and that it is offensive to women to tell them they are 'silly' to walk abroad after dark. If older women would band together (and why not their husbands too?) and would take their courage in both hands and walk sedately in considerable numbers along the dark streets where women have been harassed, mugged or even raped, it might have a remarkable effect. No man would venture to attack a company of dignified and matronly women and their walking together might bring it home to their fellow citizens that it is not somehow women's own fault if they are attacked.

6
Pursuits

With all the delightful things one can enjoy in the years of choice, there is, to my mind no doubt at all that the best way to use one's later years is a regular job. It may be paid, though probably at a lower rate than in earlier years, or it may be voluntary. The *commitment* is the thing that gives deep-down satisfaction to most of us. This chapter is about jobs, both paid and unpaid, which require regular attendance, regular fulfilment of some function. First, voluntary activity, undertaken because one hopes to benefit others. It is not sentimentality or patronizing 'do-goodism' to rate this so highly, but practical experience and sheer commonsense. Taking on a voluntary job means securing approval from one's fellows and achieving some status within the community. It means the certainty of company which we may greatly need as we quit our lifetime of paid employment, and it means involvement, which is perhaps the most important factor of all in combating ageism and the fear of growing old.

If you attend a woodwork class or a bowls club or a gramophone society, the only person who suffers if you don't turn up is yourself. But if you miss your turn on the rota for making tea at the blood transfusion centre, serving in the local hospital shop, wheeling the library trolley round the wards or manning the Samaritans' telephone, someone else is going to suffer. For the generation coming up to retirement now, *duty* is the strongest motivation and nothing is so certain to get us out of our armchairs and away from the gogglebox as the nagging consciousness that something needs to be done and we have promised to do it. It is, after all, when giving in to a cold or to feeling a bit headachy becomes 'I don't think I'll bother tonight' that we are on the slippery slope towards 'I can't get out much these days'.

People who have always fitted in some element of voluntary service move naturally from snatching a few hours a week, or even a month, away from the family and the paid job into practically full-time service on committees and councils. Those who have not made this their way of life may not find it easy to understand what satisfaction it gives or, indeed, how it can enhance one's status and the esteem of one's fellows. A woman who has never had a paid job in her life may become the national president of a women's organization, a position of far greater importance than she or her husband could probably have achieved in their bread-and-butter jobs. She will travel all over the country; she will be greeted as a beloved VIP; she will be invited to many important functions, possibly a reception at Downing St or a Buckingham Palace garden party. She may well be awarded an honour and be decorated by the Queen. Similarly, a man who has had a fairly routine job in a bank or a solicitor's office or run a small business may have had far more satisfaction in being mayor of his borough than from any of his work roles. What is more, voluntary service imposes no age limits. Many organizations rightly have rules which limit the number of years one may serve as chairman, or on a committee but we are not flung out automatically when we become sixty, seventy or even eighty. We are still needed and should never apologize for being old. Even if young committee colleagues have the edge on us for energy and up-to-date ideas we can offer experience. It is well to wait until asked for one's opinion, perhaps. Times do change, situations do alter and methods of approach now acceptable are different from those we used in our younger days. But experience brings patience, steadfastness and the invaluable quality of never being too discouraged or too upset to carry on with the good work.

In urging people to give their time and concern to voluntary organizations I don't at all want to suggest that committee work is all joy. There are hassles, there are disappointments and there are, no doubt about it, occasionally quite painful experiences. You have to have an inner reserve of strength and will-power, and a reserve, also of basic optimism — which is where the old tend to score over the young. Remember Millicent Garrett Fawcett, who started working for women's suffrage when she was a newly-wed and never faltered for half a century or more. She was eighty-one when women gained the vote on the same terms with men, in 1928. Eleanor Rathbone, an Independent MP, said that it took twenty-five years to get a reform through Parliament. She had reason to know for she campaigned steadfastly for that length of time for legislation to provide family allowances, or 'child benefit' as we now call it. Like Dame Millicent, she never gave up.

Campaigns in the news often draw an influx of lively personalities whose value is in stimulating interest and getting publicity. It is no use complaining if they pass across the sky rather like a shooting star. The 'stars' tend to take their talents elsewhere in due course and leave the hard core of the faithful still at it. There are people who can ignite a flame — perhaps because they are well known, used to taking the lead, are inspiring talkers or just naturally have charisma — and there are people who have the patience and diligence to keep that flame alight. Both kinds are needed and should respect and value each other for what they can give.

To accept that people may get hurt is essential for voluntary workers. For one reason or another regular attenders, faithful supported, may not be re-elected to a committee, be chosen as a delegate to some prestigious conference or properly thanked for their behind-the-scenes work. There are ideological conflicts, too, which seem impossible to resolve and there are personality clashes which need angelic tact and patience to cope with. Sometimes a short, sharp confrontation which brings smouldering resentment into the open clears the way for better co-operation. I have heard that a kitchen 'pinger' is a godsend to a harassed chairman unable to silence garrulous members, causing good-natured mirth as it helps the business forward. Sometimes I think the best advice I ever gave to a distressed committee member was 'Ask the chap to supper, and make sure it is a good one!'

Running a local pensioners' association, a job that naturally appeals to many who are pensioners themselves, is not much different from running any other society, but has its own special hurdles. The experience of a very old friend who involved herself for fourteen years in an organization of this kind is illuminating. For eleven years she was a committee member, for two years she was chairman and she served also for various terms as secretary, social secretary and birthdays secretary. Hers must be quite a typical story.

> There are very few members left now [she told me] who originally formed or joined our pensioners' club nineteen years ago, the causes being old age, removal from the area, increased infirmity or death. The initial intense enthusiasm has gone. I look round the membership today and scarcely know half of them by name. There was a period two years ago when the resignations of secretary, chairman and president followed upon one another. The treasurer died, as did several committee members and of a committee of twelve, only seven or eight remained. It looked as if the club might founder, but help came from a husband and wife who took over the jobs of secretary and treasurer until there was a resurgence of members' interest and officials and committee were once more elected.
>
> We are now functioning fairly successfully again, but there is an entirely new atmosphere, little concern about the club constitution and rules. All the members are concerned about is that the club gives them their weekly chance to meet together to play bingo, dominoes and whist, join outings during the summer and have a free Christmas party.
>
> The older members are content to leave things as they are. There is a memory of quite a fierce split in the club in 1965 which lasted for eleven years, with the club being denied the use of a very comfortable local hall (now regained). The main protagonists in this really awful quarrel have died or moved away from the district. What I felt — new then to the club — was that there was no point of

compromise in the affair because the characters of those involved were already well and truly fixed.

Is this a special problem or organizations run by, as well as for, elderly people? My friend thinks it is indeed a factor 'which must arise constantly in old people's relationships with one another. An enemy is an enemy is an enemy . . ..' And yet we who have lived so long should know that tolerance is one of the greatest human virtues. Some of us do seem to grow more cantankerous as we grow older, but surely not *all*? Looking back on her years with the pensioners' club my friend was anxious to stress the importance of a good chairman (of either sex) and a good committee 'formed of true zealots and lively enthusiasts for promoting friendship and goodwill. The chairman especially needs to be very capable and very tactful to keep matters running smoothly, for there are always the whisperers and moaners who can sour the atmosphere unless handled carefully.'

Another vital matter is the need for a constant influx of new members, some of whom can be persuaded to take office for a year or two. This applies not only to organizations for the elderly and newly retired but also to organisations like the Women's Institutes and Townswomen's Guilds. In the nature of things, some of the best members die and some of the others get too tired to continue carrying the responsibilities of office. In all organizations opinions differ as to whether there should be a time limit for office-bearing and committee membership. Limitation has the disadvantage that an excellent official may have to resign just as he/she is beginning to exert real leadership. But if members can hold office for ever other people tend to stop taking any interest in the

113

yearly elections and younger members may be too diffident to stand in opposition to established office bearers. It is the sign of impending death, as many an organization knows, when people are no longer willing to stand for office. Sometimes a splitting of jobs is the answer — minute secretary, correspondence secretary, membership secretary and so on. Patience as well as goodwill is needed to work out solutions which encourage the young without sacrificing the old.

It may seem that voluntary work is more readily available to women than to men. It is true that the married woman at home has found the Institute, the Guild, the Club, the Circle an outlet for her energies and even for her ambition, which men absorbed in their work life do not need. In their late years many women still have a strong commitment, a sense of being useful in a world which is new, strange and perhaps unattractive to their husbands. But it is very far from true that there is no call for ageing men in the field of voluntary work. While working on this book I have met a number of elderly men who are giving dedicated service to various organizations for the welfare of people of similar age, as well as men who have been very happy that retirement gave them time to take a greater part in the affairs of their church or club. It may be that a retired business or professional man does not take to the idea of serving behind the counter of an Oxfam, Save the Children Fund or Help the Aged charity shop. 'Women's work' he may say to himself. But all such gift shops and many other organizations need someone to 'cash up', take the money to the bank, audit the accounts and collect and deliver goods. Men who have run small businesses take to this kind of work like ducks to water and are immensely appreciated by the 'counter hands'.

The simplest way for a retired man to get involved in voluntary work may be through work for the elderly and aged, but many find it more stimulating and rewarding to work with people of all ages, on a wider range of problems. Citizens' Advice Bureaux attract a high proportion of men. Work experience of any kind provides a fund of basic 'know-how' in some field or other and usually the capacity to digest necessary information of any kind and pass it on. There is no doubt that there is a great satisfaction in being able to provide the answer to a tricky question, whether it is a TV or Radio quiz contest or over the counter at a Citizens' Advice Bureau, and there are many of us (perhaps more men than women?) who are more at ease or more skilled in dealing with facts than with feelings. There is a tremendous need for such people, for our very complicated society throws up a great many problems which our system of education does not necessarily help us to solve. The Bureaux came into being during the Second World War to help people who were bombed out, evacuated or bereaved. There are still casualties of society — people living in the middle of slum clearance schemes, people fearing loss of social security benefits, people unable to keep up high hire purchase payments, people ignorant of their rights, fearful of the law, a prey to the dishonest or the dictatorial, and, most prevalent of all, people pathetically ill-informed, muddled and inarticulate. (A friend remembers particularly vividly a widow who had somehow got hold of the idea that she was entitled to claim the return of all the income tax her husband had paid over the years.)

Citizens' Advice Bureaux volunteers are, of course, vetted by the local committee and if acceptable given a course of training, so that no one need fear being dangerously incompetent in his or her first days on the counter or at the telephone. But the immense strength of the Bureaux is the truly marvellous information service which keeps all the local offices up-to-date with changes in the law and in regulations of every kind. A Cheshire Bureau's news for one month, taken at random, not only gave information on changes in family income supplement, increases in limits for legal aid, legal advice and assistance and the cost of certain birth, marriage and death certificates, but listed forty information leaflets — on subjects as various as industrial tribunal procedure, service agents approved by the Paraffin Heating Advisory Council, the fees for naturalization and registrations and the rules about bringing animals into Great Britain.

Of special appeal to men, perhaps, is a new organisation known as REACH — the Retired Executives Action Clearing House — which found unpaid part-time employment for 300 or so people within its first six months of operation. Men fixed up with interesting and rewarding employment included a surveyor, to measure and record National Trust buildings, an accountant to keep the records of a YMCA and a fire brigade chief advising a housing society on fire prevention. I know myself of an excellent little organization which ran into dire financial difficulty because it had lacked a treasurer able to keep a watchful eye, month by month, on its accounts.

There is undoubtedly room for people with time to spare at the top end of the scale as well as on the ground floor. For many years the list of the 'great and good' compiled by the Civil Service Department to provide names for any Government Department setting up a Committee of Enquiry, a Royal Commission, or consumer advisory committees has been a sort of joke. 'Who are they, the great and good?', people have asked one another. 'How do they pick the names, except through the Old Boy Network? What qualifications do you have to have, apart from having friends in high places?' But now the procedure is quite plain. The Public Appointments Unit of the Civil Service Department has 'nomination forms' which anyone can ask for and fill in, indicating his/her areas of experiences and interests. A nominator must be found who is asked to provide a brief profile of the person he/she is nominating.

I wouldn't like to say whether this new procedure is improving the quality and widening the range of people asked to serve on public bodies but it must surely be a more democratic way of bringing in people of goodwill and grass-roots experience. A booklet recently prepared by a small group of representative women, Action Opportunities, is worth the attention of men as well as women of all ages. Called *Simple Steps to Public Life* it gives useful information about recruitment for bodies as widely different as community health councils and the Post Office Users National Council. The public bodies now popularly known as Quangos (quasi-autonomous non-governmental organizations) do need experienced people for both paid and unpaid part-time jobs. It is true that the higher your status in your career or voluntary service, the higher your 'public appointment' chances are likely to be. The first headmistress of Kidbrooke School, one of the earliest great comprehensives for girls, was recruited on her retirement both to the Press Council and to the General Optical Council — but people with some time to spare are needed all down the line, especially on the watchdog committees set up for the nationalised industries and for the Health Service.

We haven't all of us either taste or aptitude for public service, and it is an interesting and rather sad fact that the proportion of retired people who give their time to voluntary work is not higher than the proportion in any other age group. It seems that one either is or is not a joiner, a giver, a doer. However, whatever the reason, 'keeping active' after retirement is likely for very many of us to mean having some kind of regular paid job. It is what we are used to, what has always, all through our lives, given us our niche in society and provided us with friends and status. Given the 'ageism' in our society paid employment is not always easy to find for people who have, because of fixed pension ages, been made 'redundant' at sixty or sixty-five, and if the unemployment figures continue to grow it is likely to become still more difficult. But it does exist and there are organizations to help the enterprising and energetic man or woman to find it. Some Age Concern groups which are well supported financially by their local authority have an employment officer. His/her job is not an easy one in this time of increasing unemployment. Job offers by commercial firms are tending to decline and placements are more likely to be 'domestic'. The success stories of a recent twelve-month period in Lewisham, south-east London, included a technical supervisor of motor repairs, a relief matron for a charity home, a manageress for a charity shop, a cook for a hostel and a library steward.

When it comes to changing jobs women are more adaptable than men, according to one Age Concern general secretary. Men are apt to be harder to please because they tend to come in with a set idea and rather high expectations. 'I've been an engineer all my life', they may say, as if nothing less than the same line of work and the same degree of responsibility will do. But people *can* adapt if they have the will — and if the alternative is feeling bored and useless. A minor executive who applied to the Age Concern Lewisham bureau had been used to rubber-stamping decisions to pass on to other employees. In his retirement no one ever asked him anything. He had no authority and no status, but was not easy to place, having perhaps an exaggerated idea of what he might do. Most surprisingly he was placed successfully as a 'tea boy'. It was the strong sense of being needed that made him arrive at his work place very early and attend so conscientiously to his duties. If he pops into the employment office now he is apt to say, 'I can't stop. I have to be back at work.'

Years ago I knew a retired shop-keeper whose rather dominant wife made it plain that she thought he was getting under her feet at home. He found a most enjoyable job working the lift in a gentlemen's club. He was useful and appreciated and able to exchange pleasantries with the members all day long. Another post-retirement case I came upon was a civil servant who had reached the rank of 'principal'. When I met him he was serving as an usher in a Crown Court. He was most efficient in court and assiduous in attending the judge. It was evident to me that there was a tiny, most enjoyable element of play-acting in the job. People who find these stories pathetic rather than pleasing should remember that routine jobs can have their attraction if done by choice, in pleasant company and not as permanent full-time duties. Which of us has not enjoyed a stint of addressing and stuffing envelopes, in company, for a charity, a campaign, or an election?

Simple, routine tasks are what the work centres set

up by the Employment Fellowship provide, especially for the really elderly, for whom the work is definitely therapy, to prevent dangerous feelings of isolation and loss of identity. The Employment Fellowship is one of the most interesting and altruistic aspects of voluntary help for old people. Its origin goes back to the Winter Distress League of the 1920s, set up in the industrial north-east, which was described at the time as a 'sepsis point'. A former administrative officer of the Fellowship, Edward Burton, recalled to me that in the 1950s no one expected to see long-term employment ever again, so the idea was developed of providing a lifeline for the men and women who were 'unemployed' because of their age. Deprived of occupation, status and companionship, quite a number of men go quickly downhill. 'I heard of a man', said Mr Burton, 'who actually died at his retirement party, and quite a few last only a year or two. Most organizations for the elderly provided activities designed merely to fill in time. The attitude was cups of tea and sympathy. Nothing productive was offered to the old.'

The Fellowship's London office is a single room at one end of the Society of Friends building at Euston. Help the Aged provided money for fostering workshops and the Department of Health and Social Security funds the little headquarters office. The director, T.H. Oakman, who operates from Hertfordshire, the administrative officer and three regional development officers comprise the staff. They help to set up new workshops and foster and encourage them. There are now at least 200 around the country. Despite initial enthusiasm for what is obviously a good idea, actually launching a new workshop may take a long while. The proposal may have come from a councillor or other local dignitary who turns out to be unpopular on either personal or political grounds; the search for premises can be frustrating. Trade union opposition, happily, is very rare and every workshop committee aims to include an active trade unionist. One enthusiast, a master builder, started a workshop in his own dining room. When it began to overflow he went across the road and built more suitable premises himself.

Workshops are expected to be self-supporting, though some do have a local grant. Rent, rates and the salary of the organiser have to be met out of the sums paid for the job contracts, as well as the wages of the workers who participate. Organizers are usually women and their skill and devotion are truly remarkable. They have to persuade manufacturers and others to provide a steady flow of work that elderly and inexperienced people can do and to bargain for a rate of pay — one that will not exploit the workers or raise trade union hostility and yet will make this form of 'outwork' financially satisfactory to the employer. The hourly rate for the workers is far less than they could earn as domestics or gardeners, little more than pocket money, in fact, but the recognition that what they are doing has a market value is crucial.

Diversification of jobs is essential, not just to give needed variety for the workers but also so that if one manufacturer withdraws supplies of work there is always something to take its place. The story is told that the Exeter work centre survived for months on a diet of Devon violets. Actually, sweet-smelling jobs, like wrapping toilet soap, are quite common. I was able to visit a workshop in the borough of Camden, part of a day centre. It was a large sunny room with plants on the windowsills all down one side. There were thirty-eight people on the register, almost all women, and the work I saw them doing seemed particularly suitable. They were not only wrapping soap but also boxing china and stapling small scraps of brightly coloured material on to pattern-order sheets. These workers also pack denture moulds which are sent out all over the world. Age and infirmity are not necessarily a barrier to regular attendance. One regular workshop attender is ninety-one. She started work sixteen years ago and still comes on foot. At another workshop two arthritics form a team. One can make a hole and the other can push a thread through it.

But the age and infirmity of the workers do mean that the organizer has to be exceptionally dedicated to her job. This Camden centre organiser checks work fanatically. China can arrive chipped or be chipped in handling. Deliveries back to the firm must be accurate. '*Everything* has to be counted', she said woefully. 'People of this age often can't count accurately' — 'this age' means anything from sixty-seven to ninety-five. The centre is in a rather 'select' residential area, where there is no industry. It cannot call on any transport to collect or deliver work so that the chase for orders is tricky. Yet despite all her worries this organizer regards workers as a family and raises funds locally to take them on coach outings with packed lunches.

Other workshops seem to have a rather more independent membership. 'We are not afraid of hard or dirty work,' wrote the organizer of the Telford work centre, which is fortunate to have the backing of the Telford Development Corporation and serves a notable range of industries — ballbearings, car accessories, chemicals, electrical locks, packaging, plastics, rainwater goods and rubber. Selly Oak concentrates on local hospitals. Some centres actually make their own products, mostly soft and wooden toys and there have been efforts to set up a marketing group. A still more enterprising development is Sheffield Pensioner Enterprises Ltd, a company established specifically to employ people who wish to continue work after their official retirement. It has a remarkable board of directors who include the founder of several international companies, a past master cutler, past presidents of the local Chamber of Commerce and Chamber of Trade and a number of leading academics, all at least in their later sixties themselves.

Reading about some of these activities in the *Employment Fellowship Review*, a quarterly newssheet, it struck me that there was a liveliness, a kind of gaiety about the way they come across. This may be a clever public relations exercise, or it may be a rather superficial euphoria in me, but I fancy the cheerfulness is genuine. People who work in their sixties and seventies mostly work because they want to work. They are likely to work without stress, without the pressure of ambition, and without resentment about 'differentials'. (Aren't most industrial disputes nowadays about differentials — the strong feeling one group of workers has that they are worth at least as much as, and probably more than, some other group?) I myself experienced this lightness of spirit in a post-retirement job known by both sides to be short-term. The work was quite responsible and challenging but a lifetime's experience in the field made it not too taxing. My colleagues in all departments were exceptionally friendly and likeable but I think it was the lack of *long-term* responsibility that made this one of the happiest periods of my working life.

The satisfactions of work for work's sake obviously animate many of the men and women who get post-retirement jobs through the agency Success After Sixty, because the work is seldom in the senior grade the applicant has filled before retirement. The minor executive who gained satisfaction from being a 'tea boy' can be matched many times over in Success After Sixty's case books: a barrister who became a filing clerk with a merchant bank for lower pay than a bright young secretary would get or a bank manager who became a book-keeper for a firm of estate agents. This smallish organization is a division of a large commercial agency, the Career Care Group. Its range is mainly in the field of office and allied jobs and it operates only in the London area, but it is a model to be studied because of its genuine concern for older people — who are charged no fees.

Since it opened up in 1975 Success After Sixty has had about 1,500 men and women on its books and has placed a third of them. There are always more applicants than jobs available, but the main problem is matching jobs to people. The right job in Hampstead is the wrong job for a person living in Dulwich if it takes him/her at least an hour to get there by public transport. It isn't even the time and cost of travel that are the primary barrier. It is the physical wear and tear, which as many quite young commuters know, can be really burdensome, especially in bad weather, during industrial disputes or at times when services are disrupted by signal failures, repairs to lines or traffic jams on the roads.

Success After Sixty's approach to employers is purposeful and positive.

The contribution older people make is very considerable, not only in terms of hard work and punctuality but also in terms of providing balance

124

and stability in the office where they work. They are very popular with young people. A responsible attitude to their work makes them ideal staff to open and lock up offices or handle confidential accountancy work. Many of our clients have found that work done by a more mature person, not so much concerned with promotion, new clothes or where to spend holidays, is often performed with more dedication and loyalty than that given by the younger generation. Older people had time to develop those unwritten qualifications of tact, diplomacy and experience. They are rarely concerned about status.

A voluntary agency working in much the same way as Success After Sixty, Buretire is an imaginative offshoot of the Employment Fellowship. Its aim is to find employment for people who want to work in an 'open' situation rather than in sheltered workshops. Its clients are almost all seeking occupation even more than money, but there are some who still have young families to educate. We are apt to forget that there are quite a number of men who have made second marriages in their fifties who, when they come to retirement age, still have dependent children. If the concern for which they work has a rigid retirement policy their problem is likely to be grim. Sometimes it is eased by the comparatively young wife returning to work, perhaps after retraining, envisaging the time when she must be the sole breadwinner. But fathers naturally want to be breadwinners too.

By mid-1979 Buretire had five experimental projects in Reading, Walthamstow, Bishop's Stortford, Watford and London, in co-operation with Rotary. The spread of job experience among their clients is wide, and quite a high proportion are people who have held very responsible and well-paid jobs. Few are now even looking for, let alone expecting, similar top jobs. I was told of one man who though he had been an international banker and quite well-known economist had a fancy to work as a forecourt attendant. He tried it for six months but, not surprisingly, didn't find it sufficiently mentally stimulating. He moved on quite happily to the supervision and control of a leisure centre at £60 a week.

It was surprising — though it should not really have been — to learn that some of Buretire's clients are referred to them by doctors. Loneliness, loss of status and meaningful occupation can have a disastrous effect on physical as well as mental health. As Mr Reg Birks of Buretire, Bishop's Stortford, said to me:

> People who listen a good deal to radio and watch TV are apt to pick up information which leads them to imagine they may have the symptoms of serious illness. Men who have been in positions of authority are particularly at risk . . . and of course they all have friends and relations who have died in their fifties, let alone their sixties, of coronaries. To put it bluntly, men who are now at home twenty-four hours a day can be a thorough nuisance to their wives. Sometimes it is the goodnatured wife who suffers most by being told, in her husband's accustomed authoritarian manner, what to do, as if she were one of his employees. But sometimes it is the husband himself who has a rough time, if the wife is a fairly dominant character who makes him aware that he is under her feet and a source of extra work for her, rather than a welcome partner and companion.

Such a man feels his loss of status doubly; he is no longer of importance because of his work and is little more than an interloper in the domestic economy of his home.

Buretire seeks to provide preventives rather than cures for such ills. It is run by volunteers in little offices let for very low rent by health centres, YMCAs and building societies and staffed for only two or three hours a day. The 'manager' has to be out and about, interesting potential employers in his clients. Mr Birks finds, he told me, that sometimes older men and women are very useful in being able to pass on helpful business contacts to new firms run by younger people. And almost always older people are prepared to work the unsocial hours that are such a source of grievance to many younger people. They don't at all mind opening up a newsagent's shop to receive the morning papers at 6.30 a.m. or manning the telephone at a school for the handicapped from 5.30 to 10.30 p.m. Jobs that young people are loth to do, whatever the pay, are often acceptable to the elderly. Buretire's initial success has persuaded the organizers to draft plans to open up 200 offices by 1983. They hope to get help not only from Rotary Clubs but from trades councils, chambers of commerce, chambers of trade and the like. The bureaux need to be pretty well self-supporting. Fees are charged to employers, but on a very modest scale, as practically all the jobs are part-time.

Interesting and promising schemes operating in the United States are described in an excellent book *Young Till We Die* by Doris and David Donas. *Late Start* was sponsored by the National Retired Teachers Association and the American Association of Retired Persons. The project WORK (Wanted Older Residents with Know-how) succeeded in placing more than fifty applicants in productive work in Long Beach, California. The Green Thumb programme set up by the National Farmers Union with a grant from the Department of Labour, permitted the 'elderly poor' to earn up to $1,500 a year by working three days a week. During 1970 more than 1,400 of them improved or built more than 350 roadside parks, planted more than a million trees, flowers and shrubs, cleaned out lakes, built picnic places and helped to restore and develop historical sites. One eighty-eight-year-old man commented with a grin, 'Those boys left me — the name of the one was Arthur and the second Ritus. It means arthritis was in my arms. I believe Green Thumb is the reason I am living today.'

Doris and David Donas propound an excellent idea for making use of the skills of the elderly for everyone's benefit — 'Mr Fixit shops'. 'Our daily convenience is at the mercy of a growing armada of gadgets and appliances. If a small cog in their wheels is loose, the result is a total standstill, with no alternative means.' As these authors say, manufacturers will repair gadgets up to a point, but what we sorely need is local repair shops on a large scale. 'Why not offer inducements to private industry to set up a parent agency to offer financing and know-how to regional centres which it would licence?' they ask. Such regional centres, it is suggested, could provide workshops, warehouses and reception centres and recruit elderly persons of both kinds: 'Workers qualified by lifetime experience; those able to teach skills, managers and office workers; and the unskilled willing to be trained.' It sounds a workable scheme, but I have not heard any news of developments.

In Great Britain a project with a somewhat similar

aim, Mutual Aid Centres, set up by Michael Young (Lord Young), founder of the Consumer Association, seems to have considerable possibility of developing into a service provided by as well as for the elderly. Its multi-purpose community workshop in Hackney re-conditions a wide variety of small electrical items and furniture — the things one hates to throw away but cannot as a rule get anyone to repair. The jobs are done, at present, by unemployed young trainees who are selected through the Manpower Services Commission — but the men who train them in these invaluable skills are very experienced older men, not yet of pensionable age, but nearing it. Obviously retired craftsmen could play a most important part in running such workshops, which also intend to provide a call-out repair service for the housebound and disabled and a 'do-it-yourself' workshop on their premises.

The need to get small jobs done about the house presses especially severely on ageing people who, even if they can get an expert to come to the house, find the going rate of pay difficult to afford. This has led many people to think in terms of skill-swapping groups, especially widows and widowers who used to have a partner who would mend a jacket pocket or change plugs and replace fuses. People without partners can and often do learn to do a wide range of domestic tasks, but some still defeat many of us. This was the thinking behind Link Opportunity, set up originally by Edward Walton of Age Concern in 1975 as 'a contribution to two of old age's worst problems, inactivity and poverty'. The basic idea was job-swapping, in the form of barter by tokens instead of money. Many of us have a sneaky feeling that money (not only 'the love of money') is the root of a lot of evil and that if we could get back to exchanging our products and our skills we should be a lot happier. On a large scale this is an impossible dream, of course, in a Western industrialized society, but for those who are no longer in the rat race, couldn't it be made to work to a useful degree?

Many people believe it could. By spring 1979 there were estimated to be thirty Link Opportunity schemes around the country, bringing together about 2,000 people — absurdly few considering the 9,000,000 people drawing retirement pensions, and that everyone, who is told about Link's job-swap basis says, 'What a splendid idea. Why hasn't it spread like wildfire?' The method is similar to the baby-sitting rota plan. The young mother notches up a credit of the number of hours she spends minding some other mother's children and can call on any mother member of the rota to 'pay her back' by sitting with *her* children. Link members are issued with a card and, usually, a number of stamps as a starter, each representing an hour's service from other members of the group. Mr Smith puts in two hours mowing Mrs Jones's lawn and gets two stamps. Mrs Jones may not be a very good needlewoman, but Mrs Robinson will gladly accept one of Mr Smith's credit stamps in payment for an hour spent mending his socks and Mrs Jones one for baking Mr Smith a pie. And so it should happily go on. But it isn't quite so simple in practice as everyone wishes it were. Mr Smith and Mrs Brown and Mrs Robinson may all be able to manage most of their domestic jobs quite successfully. What they really need may be a handy chap with an electric drill, a competent plumber or an accountant to help with their income tax, who never seem to materialize. It is rather like the Success After Sixty situation —

plenty of people willing to offer their skills and quite a few jobs needing to be done, but matching them up is much harder than one would expect.

In fact I gather that though stamps affixed to a card to indicate work done and an entitlement to repayment in kind seem a splendid idea, they aren't necessarily very important in job-swaps except to people who naturally like collecting stamps, tokens and such. I learned a lot by spending a few hours in Bath in the company of Isabel Groves, organizer of one of the most successful Link schemes. She sees it very much as running an extended family. 'In a genuine, close-knit family,' she says, 'everyone contributes something. Mum does the baking. Dad does the painting and decorating, grandfather weeds the garden and little Johnny runs errands for Granny, who in turn knits him a smart school pullover. Auntie down the road is available for baby-sitting. That is precisely the sort of atmosphere we try to create in Link.' By and large Bath succeeds in this idealistic aim. How? In the first place it gives fascinating unpaid 'employment' to a score of volunteers, mostly women of mature years if not actually retired. They staff the office five days a week, from 10 a.m. through to 4 a.m., in three two-hourly shifts. The rota is kept immaculately and deputies are alerted promptly in case of need. Every call, in person or by phone, is listed in a log book. The office is in a pleasant small room on the premises of the Manvers Street Church Hall, just near Bath station and is excellently signposted. It is quite separate from all the other activities in the church hall and so can create its own atmosphere, which Isabel Groves thinks is important. The room was furnished entirely with gifts, including a carpet from the local Chamber of Commerce.

One of this Link scheme's notions is a well-set-out alphabet of job skills available. It goes from antique valuing to window-cleaning, by way of a locksmith, a masseur, a business adviser, and a plumber; also people willing to help with income tax, small electrical jobs, car repairs, car washing, upholstery, chess, letter-writing, china mending and trumpet tuition. One of the difficulties about job-swapping is that people know well what they need but cannot imagine what they have to offer. And of course we come up against the imbalance of the sexes in later years — there are far more women able to offer cooking and sewing than men able to offer digging and carpentering. This is one of the reasons why Mrs Groves thinks the involvement of younger people is so important. The young benefit, too. A young man who gave up his evenings to decorate an invalid's sitting room was surprised and delighted to be offered free use of a caravan for a week. The lad who cheerfully volunteered to mow lawns got a crash course in French just before setting off on a continental holiday.

It wouldn't be surprising if the people who get the most out of Bath's Link are the voluntary staff. Certainly it must give great pleasure to those who are 'fixers' by nature and inclination to be able to find just the person to meet a need. Imagine being rung up by a mother desperate to find someone to put a patch on the inner tube of her son's bicycle and to be able to offer instant help; or sorting out a woman equally desperate to find someone to disentangle her knitting; or someone so dreadfully agitated by her dog having fits that she calls up to beg for someone to sit with her until the vet arrives. An arthritic in Bath who could do most things for herself except pull on her stocking wanted someone to live on the premises. She was fixed up with a woman who actually arrived hopefully with her sheets and stayed on. In its first eighteen months Bath Link put about 250 people in touch.

Why have other groups not been so successful? It is difficult to find satisfactory explanations. The excellent Age Concern group at Lewisham, south-east London, a notably caring borough, has never been able to fathom how it was that all the effort put into launching a Link Opportunity scheme came to nothing. Edward Walton, the 'inventor' of the idea, helped to set it up; the Social Service department was keen; the Mayor chaired a public meeting and an excellent steering committee was formed with representatives from the Inner London Education Authority, pensioners organizations, adult education associations and others. A thousand Link stamps were ordered and the telephone number was publicized by press and radio. The result of all this was just three enquiries.

So the organizers, experienced and dedicated social workers, tried again. They chose a couple of quite different areas in the borough and recruited students to saturate them with leaflets. They contacted nearly 800 households between them — but only four people showed interest. Eventually the scheme was put into cold storage. It was a bitter and baffling disappointment for organizers who had so much deserved success. Another disappointing story came to me from Gateshead, which got off originally to a very good start. The Age Concern organizer built up a file of over a hundred volunteers, with a core of twenty-five workers whose services were frequently sought for gardening, decorating and small repair jobs. Unfortunately this organizer had a spell of bad health and had to give up. She had had a very close personal relationship with her volunteers and had relied upon this rather than on careful record keeping so that when she left (as did Age Concern's organizing secretary for Metropolitan Gateshead, also through ill-health) it was difficult for Link to keep going. All the hundred volunteers were circularized by the chairman and asked to write or call in if they wished to continue with the scheme. There were only two positive responses. The chairman thought that a high proportion of the original volunteers were really elderly and did not feel able to offer 'active service' any longer. Certainly Gateshead's experience adds weight to the view that Link needs a spread of age groups as well as of skills.

It seems to me, also, that the personality of the leader or leaders may be a crucial factor. Most paid staff are just as dedicated and at least as reliable as volunteers, but they do not always have the same flexibility. Isabel Groves in Bath believes that one of the most important jobs she does for Link is going round and talking about it — to Women's Institutes, Townswomen's Guilds, church women's meetings, women's clubs, in fact any group that will invite her. This is partly to keep up the interest and to recruit participants and partly to raise funds. She offers these groups the carrot of a 'super pre-Christmas party'. 'They pay 20p a head,' says Mrs Groves, 'but we give them a smashing tea and the function raises £50 to £60. We need the money. We only pay a small rent but the telephone is a great expense.' Telephone calls cannot be stinted when it is a matter of finding someone to answer an urgent cry for help. So there are monthly coffee mornings in supporters' homes as well as the main fund-raising event.

Bath is probably lucky in being a small, compact, homogeneous old city with a long tradition of citizen involvement. It must be much easier to get people together for a community project there than in a London borough with a large immigrant population or with a seepage to the outer suburbs. But one comes back to the realization that the ability to inspire others is an essential part of making voluntary efforts work. If Mrs Groves had to give up, as the Gateshead organizer had to give up, how easily could she be replaced? The combination of efficiency, time to spare, dedication, leadership and what one can only call a loving heart is as rare as it is precious.

7
Politics

People need politics — the art/science/methodology of getting things done by and for a community. The politics of catering for the 9,000,000 of us in the United Kingdom who are now pensioners are fascinating. Thousands upon thousands of people, paid professionals and goodhearted volunteers, are engaged in the job of helping us to run our own lives — or that is what it seems like. They sit together in committees in Whitehall, in your local town or county hall, in Mitcham, Surrey (Age Concern), in Dover St, London (Help the Aged) or in Bedford Square, London (the National Council for Voluntary Organizations, better known as the National Council for Social Service) to decide policies for what we, the sixty-plus people, need and want.

Some of these admirable people are sixty-plus themselves — including a high proportion of the fighting organizations like Pensioners' Voice (the National Federation of Old Age Pensioners' Associations), pensioners' trade union action associations and the British Association of Retired Persons — but many of those who actually run the executive committees and offices of organizations concerned with the elderly are well below pension age. Isn't it as well that we who are conscious of ageing should take a sharp look at what they are, those bodies whose stated aim is to further and protect our interests, at who runs them, at what precisely they aim to achieve, and at what policies they endorse and campaign for?

Not surprisingly, the first organized groups concerned with pensioners sprang up among pensioners themselves — the workers who were feeling the pinch of poverty far more acutely than any of our fellow citizens feel it today. These people united 'to call attention to the plight of the aged poor'. The seed of a national pensioners' association was sown in Urmston, just outside Manchester, in 1938 by a Mr J. Simmons. It is not surprising, either, that the impetus for action came from Lancashire, for it suffered sorely in the Depression of the 1930s and it had a long radical tradition. (A little earlier Miss Florence White made a considerable impact with her 'Pensions for Spinsters at 55' campaign in Lancashire.) Mr Simmons, an Urmston citizen, Mr S.C. Shaw, and a local magistrate, Mr J.C. Birtles, came together in a waiting room at London Rd station, Manchester, and took the decision to form a national organization of pensioners. This was actually born at the YMCA, Tottenham Court Rd, London, in March 1939, at a meeting which decided to ask the Government to increase the pension from 10 shillings a week to £1. The Prime Minister replied chillingly that every penny in the national exchequer was then needed for rearmament — understandably, perhaps, in this post-Munich year.

But the British electorate were shocked by what the National Federation had to tell them about the nature of the poverty of at least 1,000,000 elderly people. The petition which the Federation drafted calling for the pension to be raised was signed by 6,000,000 voters and had to be delivered to the

House of Commons in a furniture van. This was probably the largest number of signatures ever collected by any British pressure group. It did not bring an immediate increase in the pension — war was upon us — but it did undoubtedly influence the final abolition of the Poor Law in 1940 and the decision to raise Public Assistance payments and the coal allowance. Once the war was over the National Federation stepped up its pressure, and in 1946 a Labour Government increased the pension, for the first time since 1919 — from 10 shillings to 26 shillings a week for a single person and 42 shillings for a couple.

These were days of hope for the old. One can remember the lifting of fear from parents and parents-in-law who had grown up with the image of the workhouse always in mind. Without doubt the way the Second World War involved citizens, through widespread bombing and through evacuation, gave a great shake-up to received ideas about the socially deprived. In 1940 the National Council of Social Service set up the National Old People's Welfare Council. The Nuffield Foundation instituted a study of the needs of the elderly in 1944; its report, published in 1947, became a classic and resulted in the setting up of the National Corporation for the Care of Old People. In 1943 the Beveridge Report was published and laid the foundation on which the British Welfare State is constructed.

The first Labour Government to have an overall majority practically revolutionized social provision. The Beveridge concept was that benefits should depend entirely on *need* — inability through age, infirmity, unemployment or sickness to provide for oneself. The Government then accepted responsibility for providing maintenance for all in their later years (though actual pensions were contributory and so were not then payable to the very old, who had not been able to join the contributory pensions scheme in their employed days). There were obvious holes in the network of social welfare provision. There are still holes — but there are now powerful nationwide pressure groups to urge that they should be plugged. There is no possibility now of a return of those twenty-seven bitter years of the ten-bob-a-week pension. By law now the Government has to undertake an annual review of pensions. The workhouse has at last been truly demolished. If people are still afraid of old age, it is because they fear infirmity, not starvation. In the United Kingdom nowadays no one *needs* to go hungry — though probably some of the very old or very isolated people do, because they do not know what benefits are available to them or how to claim them, or because buying and preparing food have become too difficult for them to bother.

The cost of providing for the nation's 9,000,000 pensioners is a staggering £10,000 million a year — £6,000 million in pensions and supplementary benefits and £4,000 million in various subsidies, housing, tax allowances, hospital care and so on. Noughts are mind-boggling, so £10,000 million needs to be compared with the billions the country allocates to defence. Nevertheless, I believe that people entering their sixties need to look at what is provided for them out of taxes and voluntary effort and to ask themselves whether the State still treats retired people shabbily, whether the very old and frail are still at risk, and if so why, and whether they themselves feel the need of support from society over and above the statutory provision.

It is not for one who entered her seventies in good health and able to live an energetic life and to supple-

ment her pension by writing, to imply, even accident-
ally, that special social services for the elderly are not
always really needed by the sixty to seventy age
group. But I do think that all of us who are newly
retired or about to retire should give thought to our
position in society, as well as to our own personal
future. Are we inclined to say, 'I have jolly well earned
my pension and I have an unquestioned right to it'?
This is true in every sense except actuarially. It is true,
too, that we pay income tax on our pensions and we
pay rates on our homes, even if all that is coming into
our establishment is the one pension and a bit over,
whereas a property of the same rateable value may be
inhabited by several high wage-earners — father,
mother and grown-up children, perhaps. But the main
source of our income is the national exchequer. We
are, in fact, now taking more than we give. I personally
do not at all like the idea of being a dependent on
society and I think that all of us in our lively and
healthy sixties should ask ourselves whether we want
to be cosseted by social workers and given treats
and outings by well-intentioned organizations. Do we
like the thought that when Government departments
and social welfare organizations hold conferences and
publish discussion documents they are talking about
us, as well as about the really old and frail? We are
part of the Problem, whether we accept the fact or
not. I put forward these ideas at this point because I
believe it is important to accept that what the major
organizations are doing, they are doing for *us.* Is it
what we want or need? Is it what we may want or
need ten years on?

Probably the best-known organization in the field
is Age Concern, with its 1,300 local groups manned
by concerned and caring people. Its director, David

Hobman, is an able, lively-minded and energetic man, a highly successful publicist and a fluent and convincing talker. It is not surprising to learn that he thought first of becoming a lawyer and then for a while was involved in the theatre. He was still a young man, though, when he began his commitment to voluntary work, in the Forest of Dean. This led on to various jobs with the National Council of Social Service and then to the establishment of a small voluntary agency, the Social Work Advisory Service. In his late thirties David Hobman began to think it was time he 'said his own speeches' — he had written plenty for other people to deliver — and he felt ready to tackle a really big job.

It was then I happened to see the advertisement for the Old People's Welfare Council. It could, I think, just as easily have been an advertisement for the National Association of Mental Health or the National Council for the Disabled. I didn't have any particular commitment to the elderly then. I just felt it was time I took on a major national agency. It had, in my terms, to be one that would offer a combination of social welfare and social advocacy and one that was operating in the central area.

Hobman was, he says frankly, a professional — a professional communicator. He saw his job as being in charge of a small organization with a big cause, for at that time, he reckons, the elderly were very much in the shadows. No mainstream politicians had yet taken up their cause. So he gave himself five years to transform the nature of the organization and calculated he would either do it or be sacked. 'The problem now', he says with his engaging grin, 'is that I actually believe

141

my own speeches. I really believe that the care of the elderly is among the major social challenges facing society.'

There are pensioners, dyed-in-the-wool trade unionists mostly, who stoutly deny that people like David Hobman, the professionals, really speak for the pensioners themselves. One chairman of a pensioners and trade union action association actually said in a letter to me that the professionals 'tend to talk *at* pensioners, not with them' and that their main concern is 'their own large salaries — partly paid by public money'. But in fact David Hobman is little more sympathetic to the patronizing old-style philanthropic approach than is this trade unionist. When he joined the National Association for the Welfare of Old People, as it then was, he saw at first

> a voluntary body with a long tradition of care which had been far ahead of its time in the field of training volunteers but still had about it the ring of middle-class philanthropy — that is to say, privileged, caring and compassionate people tended to decide what other people needed and they set about doing it. The providers knew all about godliness and holiness and cleanliness and welfare and so they provided welfare services — but very much on *their* terms. It was an elitist sort of approach.

This was not what David Hobman wanted. His aim was to form an agency which actually went out and asked the consumer what he wanted, rather than making assumptions. He says frankly that because of this research a lot of policies developed which he personally would not have pursued. He is a person, though, who likes to operate within a firm framework of agreed policy – and when he started to look through the Association's minute books he could not really discover what its policy was. The National Old People's Welfare Council was, and still is, an amalgam of many associations; it has, in fact, sixty organizations in membership, ranging from small charities and individual churches, to the Confederation of British Industry and the Trades Union Congress, the Race Relations Board and the Equal Opportunities Commission. It is essentially a co-ordinating body and such amalgams are in danger of trying to become all things to all men. The end – that people should be served better – tends to be confused with the means, the mechanism.

So the new director's first pressing task was the formulation of an agreed national policy. It took about six years to complete even the first stage.

We took transport, income maintenance, health and housing, and on each of these subjects we went out to the people, using different techniques. We asked 2,500 pensioners about income maintenance, for example, employing professionals to ask the questions, and we formulated our policies according to the answers that came in. People didn't always like our methods. Whatever area we moved into we challenged or threatened a new set of people. When we moved into health, doctors said, 'Why didn't you stick to transport? You were doing so well there.' When we moved into housing, the housing managers said, 'Why don't you stick to health?' But as time goes on the specialists see how you can become an ally, and that the better we do our job, showing the nature and the extent of the need, the better it is for those trying to meet it.

All this policy research and discussion resulted in a document, *The National Policy,* which contains no fewer than 127 clauses. These range from major statements like 'Every person has a right to a warm and well-lit home. No one should be excluded from adequate lighting and heating in their dwellings as a result of excessive cost', to 'Age Concern believes that more seats should be provided at rail stations for persons waiting for trains and meeting others.' It is a document well worth reading and one which could provide endless discussion among groups of retired people.

Alongside the need to define policy, Age Concern's new director felt a need to examine its structure. The great and abiding strength of Age Concern is that it has at least 100,000 volunteers who actually go and visit lonely old people, help to provide meals, or in some way or another give direct service. They run the 'pop-in parlours', the visiting schemes, the street wardens, the escort service for people who have been discharged from hospital, possibly at short notice, on a Friday, when it is difficult for any patient who lives alone to arrange to have food in the house and a fire lighted. Such volunteers also run the Link Opportunity schemes, the craft and gift shops, and are great fund-raisers.

One London borough Age Concern group I visited listed some of its activities in a recent annual report:

Our social work team has concentrated this year on exploring and developing group work with the elderly. We now have groups for the bereaved and for the isolated and handicapped. We have also pioneered group work in warden-controlled flatlets . . .. Through our community work section we have encouraged a group of elderly people to 'know their

144

rights'. This group made a film on welfare rights and produced a leaflet *3 Rs for Retirement.* They are now forming themselves into an information service for the elderly . . .. We have started a new project 'Skills at home', to encourage the housebound and to use and develop handicraft skills.

This Age Concern's senior social worker reports on 281 visits paid during a year to their 'clients', on the organization of holidays for 165 elderly women and groups in several parts of the borough to give the residents an opportunity to discuss their problems and share experiences, to break down the feeling of isolation and help to build up a sense of community within the warden-supervised flatlets. Local groups like this can apply to Age Concern's headquarters for grants from the 'Operation Enterprise' fund to help in specific projects to a limit of £750 (and an overall limit of £5,000 a month).

Chronologically, the second major organization concerned with ageing people is the much less widely known Centre for Policy on Ageing, until recently called the National Corporation for the Care of Old People, and known by its initials, NCCOP. It is less well known largely because it has no branches or local groups of any kind. Its quiet purpose-built building in the grounds of Nuffield Lodge, Regents Park, London, is a power-house for the whole complex of organizations for the care of the elderly and aged, including Government departments. It emerged as a result of the report on old people undertaken by Seebohm Rowntree in 1940 and published in 1947 at the request of the Nuffield Foundation. So powerful was the impact of that report that the Foundation decided to fund further research and also to set up experimental projects. In its own words, the CPA, as one now has to learn to call it, is 'an organization established to think about problems and policies . . . a small centralized organization without local branches or groups'. A recent secretary, Hugh Mellor, thought that it is an advantage that the CPA doesn't have to 'service' local groups, since it can devote all its time, thinking and resources to stimulating and annotating research and initiating new projects.

From the CPA, with its admirable library, comes an impressive flow of information about articles, theses, research projects and books on every possible aspect of the ageing process, about the lives of the retired, the elderly and the aged, about the services which society provides for them and the needs which are not yet fully met. It publishes a bi-monthly service *New Literature on Old Age,* which monitors the field in staggering detail, and not by any means only in the United Kingdom. Following one another in a 1979 issue were references to 'Unblocking beds: a geriatric unit's experience with transferred patients', and 'The therapeutic role of cat mascots with a hospital-based geriatric population.' The CPA also publishes an annual register of social research on old age which is widely used as a reference book.

The CPA's income runs at £60,000 from the Nuffield Foundation, £60,000 from the Hayward Foundation and £55,000 from investments — enough to employ a staff of about fifteen at Nuffield Lodge and to fund important research. It has always taken a special interest in housing. Its publication in 1973 of *Housing in Retirement* and a university project funded by the Centre, *New Housing for the Elderly,* broke new ground, in giving authoritative comments from the *users* of specially designed dwellings for old people.

It set up the first national housing association for the elderly, the Hanover Housing Association, which now provides over 4,000 dwellings and has become independent. Three members of the CPA staff are concerned with 'homes' and an important part of their work is to advise on the improvement and modernization of residential homes. The use of room-dividers to give residents a greater degree of privacy was a recent subject of study.

One of the Centre's latest research projects has been transport — how to get rather incapacitated elderly people to and from health centres and doctors' surgeries. The co-ordination of transport to and from centres concerned with health is the most urgent need, but Hugh Mellor said, 'We are deeply concerned about the plight of those who do not have access to cars and cannot use public transport. We believe far more should be done to mobilize community transport resources to enable such people to attend clubs, go shopping, make social visits and obtain essential services'. A study in Birmingham showed that well over 1,000,000 trips a year were organized by 190 voluntary bodies, using 1,008 volunteers driving their own cars, 122 vehicles owned by voluntary bodies and 100 hired vehicles. But many of the vehicles, said Hugh Mellor, 'were hopelessly under-used — perhaps a vehicle might be owned by a youth club or a school and be scarcely used even for one trip a day'. The CPA believes that 'the pool of volunteer drivers has hardly been tapped yet — with the result that many disabled and frail people remain permanently housebound. This is obviously a service in which volunteer drivers who are themselves retired can play an invaluable role.'

If the Centre for Policy on Ageing is the quietest

and least well known of the large organizations concerned with the elderly, Help the Aged is probably the best known, because of its frequent and often very moving advertisements. In some ways it is the most interesting of these bodies because though its purpose is wholly charitable it is run like a large-scale business, on strictly commercial lines. Its history seems so unlikely that it is worth relating. It was a development from the Oxford Committee for Famine Relief, which was formed in 1942 to relieve the plight of starving Greeks by a prosperous business man, Cecil Jackson Cole, and others. Mr Jackson Cole had a small business in Oxford, and from this he provided the personnel to launch the appeal which soon became familiar as Oxfam and now is known round the world as one of Britain's most effective charities. He must have been an extraordinary man (he died in August 1979, at the age of seventy-seven), for he determined quite early to give his life to the Christian aims of 'healing the sick, clothing the naked and feeding the hungry' and he set about this on the basis of running his charities exactly as he ran his businesses, and his businesses as if their sole purpose were to make money for his charities. He actually advertised for Christian and public-spirited staff willing to work with him, and workers were plainly told that a major part of the company profits would be put into charitable enterprises. Business staff were given time off to work in the charities.

After Oxfam, Mr Jackson Cole's next enterprise was Voluntary and Christian Aid, launched in 1953. This helped social service organizations, including TocH, to raise funds, and it was under this umbrella that in 1962 he launched Help the Aged. This organization differs from the other great organizations for helping the elderly in one fundamental respect — its basis is that though charity may begin at home, it must not stay there. Like all Jackson Cole's charities, its ethic is firmly rooted in his Christian faith and its practice is to follow strictly business principles for the raising of large funds. The staff he and his associates engaged were appointed for their skill as fund-raisers. His followers and successors follow the same code and are cast in the same mould. They are totally committed to the Christian ideal of helping the deprived around the world and equally committed to hard business efficiency.

There was a time when a newspaper described Cecil Jackson Cole as a millionaire tycoon who dominated his charitable enterprises. Hugh Faulkner, the present director of Help the Aged, denies that this was true and stresses that Jackson Cole certainly did not live like a rich man. He had a flat in St Leonards and when in London lived 'above the shop' — in a flat at the top of the Help the Aged offices in Dover St. He had a three-piece suite in this modest apartment, which he bought, as he told everyone who visited him there, for £12 in the gift shop below. He bought his suits from the gift shop, too. Hugh Faulkner saw him one day with a label stuck on the lapel of his jacket and asked why. 'Oh, I haven't paid for it yet', said Jackson Cole, 'and I'm not taking off the label until I've paid.' This very retiring man gave only one newspaper interview in his life, and despite the immense influence he had on the social welfare scene, only a handful of people in the welfare organizations have ever heard his name.

Hugh Faulkner is quite a remarkable man himself, very much in the Jackson Cole mould. If his family had been able to afford to send him to the Birmingham

School of Music when Granville Bantock was keen to have him as a student, he would probably have become a professional pianist. Music remains an important part of his life; his wife is a professional cellist and their daughter studied at the Royal Academy of Music. Failing a career in music young Hugh Faulkner took a job in educational administration in Leicester. During the Second World War he was a conscientious objector and for ten years was secretary of the Fellowship of Reconciliation, a Christian peace organization. He then joined Jackson Cole in one of his businesses.

Business and organization have been my interest [he says categorically]. I am not a sociologist and am not really a person who has got involved in caring for people in a professional way. My aim, and the fundamental aim of Help the Aged, is to campaign and raise funds to enable other people to do the job and to support those who are good at it, whether they are ordinary folk who are being good neighbours or are consultant geriatricians . . . as in the housing field. When we decided to go into housing we set up a housing association, so that those of us who were raising the funds didn't get caught up in running the scheme — there were others who were trained for that. We take that view still. One of the toughest jobs that has to be done is raising the wherewithal to get things done. We don't want to get diverted from it. It is much easier to go visiting and so forth than to get the money, and skills have to be developed for this task. Funds have been steadily, even spectacularly increasing in recent years, despite the nation's economic difficulties.

It is necessary to look at the fund-raising operation

as honestly and as unsentimentally as Hugh Faulkner and his Board of Trustees do. The charity employs, at the time of writing, nearly 450 people, at a cost of £976,700 in salaries and so on. Living off the backs of the beneficiaries? Hardly. Those fund-raisers between them gathered in £7,250,000 in one year, and £5,500,000 of it was spent on Help the Aged projects. The Youth Campaign alone has a staff of over a hundred, who visit schools and put on events. In one year this campaign raised more than £1,250,000. Another group of forty people is engaged in raising money and collecting clothing for overseas. They work from their own homes and organize appeals through churches and other local bodies. Other fund-raisers are real specialists who know, when money is needed for some special project, which trusts, business houses and so on can be approached hopefully.

Every aspect of Help the Aged's operations has to be cost-effective. Hugh Faulkner says, 'Every one of those advertisements you see in your newspaper has a key so that we know how much money each pulls in. It is watched on a daily basis and if the advertisement isn't working as it should it is stopped.' Business standards are applied rigidly, even toughly. 'I'm tougher in charity than I am in business', says Faulkner, 'because it is other people's money. Business belongs to the company, and if the company is content not to make a profit, that is its own decision. But a charity that is not doing its work on a reasonable expense basis has to be looked at extremely seriously. One is accountable not only to the public but to one's own conscience.'

There are other ways in which Help the Aged is run as a business — in its risk-taking and its firm allocation of responsibility. Faulkner asserts, as did Jackson

Cole, that if an organization never takes risks, breaking new ground, fostering new projects, it stagnates. Strangely enough, the organization does not have a national fund-raising committee. The responsibility lies with one person alone. It used to lie with Cecil Jackson Cole and when he died it passed to Hugh Faulkner, 'until', as he said, 'we can find someone else. The job is like that of the managing director of a business. He either does it or he doesn't, and if he doesn't he is out.' Though he was the founder of Help the Aged it is on record that when Cecil Jackson Cole took over the job of being responsible for fund-raising he laid down conditions. One was that he would raise the percentage every year by an acceptable figure. If he didn't, the trustees would say 'Out' to him, and on those terms the honorary appointment was scrutinized every year.

Works which Help the Aged has funded are, of course, very often abroad — in India, Latin America and the Far East. It channels a great deal of aid into countries devastated by floods, cyclones, earthquakes, volcanic erruptions and every other natural disaster, but the work of raising money to relieve poverty, malnutrition and disease never ceases. Help the Aged now has a special team of about thirty people raising funds for India inside India and obviously they can raise substantially more than could be sent out from the United Kingdom. At home Help the Aged has funded day centres for the active, and day hospital and rehabilitation units. Research aid includes the study of blood degeneration in the aged, the preventative aspects of ageing and the causes of senile dementia. Practical aid funded includes a chiropody unit. It is not a surprise to learn that there is almost always a very generous response to special appeals —

as, for instance, calls for help for the Boat People or the starving refugees of Kampuchea — but the people who tend to send cheques, says Hugh Faulkner, are the older people on fixed incomes. The 'newly well off' — the highly skilled and well-paid wage-earners — haven't yet got the habit of pulling out their cheque books when they are moved. If you appeal to them through their children, who ask to be 'sponsored' for something, the response is immediate and generous.

There are then three major strands in the web of voluntary provision for the elderly, old and aged: the fund-raisers, Help the Aged; the researchers, the Centre for Policy on Ageing; and the providers of direct, personal care (what is now chillingly referred to by sociologists as 'service delivery'), Age Concern. Those of us who are newly retired are apt to look with distaste on the development of all those high-powered organizations and wonder whether the study of gerontology and the care of the aged has not become one of the notable 'growth industries' (between 1976 and 1980 the U.S. Gerontological Society has information on 4,000 PhD theses on ageing). So, for our part, we should go along with David Hobman of Age Concern, who says emphatically that his organization has recognized that it should concentrate its resources on *the very old.* 'The young retired', he asserts, 'are a resource. They should not be the done-by; they should be the doers. We should concentrate, as a welfare agency on the most vulnerable, the most isolated, the 2,000,000 over 75 who live alone. We know where to find them now; we know who they are. The most vulnerable member of the community today will be an old woman, a widow probably, living alone.' Help the Aged's Hugh Faulkner has put it equally forcefully, 'Only those whose health will not allow a continu-

153

ation of work or active retirement should really be eligible for putting their feet up and doing nothing.'

If we can absolve the organizations concerned with the old from living off our backs and dancing attendance on people who neither need nor want it, can we also absolve them from overlapping in their activities? The Centre for Policy on Ageing has produced a useful little leaflet, *One Cause,* which briefly outlines the work of the three national organizations and both shows how they dovetail and reveals how they operate assiduously in some of the same fields. All produce their own literature, information sheets, reports and so on. Help the Aged has an excellent monthly newspaper for pensioners called *YOURS,* formerly circulated free to at least 1,000,000 people. This was obviously a very expensive operation and members of the committee jibbed and pointed out that the money spent on free distribution could feed large numbers of people in India. (Hugh Faulkner admitted, 'There was a bit of tension about this. I asked the Department of Health and Social Security if they could help us in any way and was smartly turned down, though they thought the newspaper was a very good thing.')

YOURS is now sold at 10p a copy. Naturally this greatly reduced the circulation though it soon crept back up to 300,000. At this time feelers were being put out for selling *YOURS* through newsagents and bookstalls, but Hugh Faulkner was firmly of the opinion that delivery of the paper to the door by volunteers was the very best way of keeping a tactful eye on the isolated old and frial. 'I really don't like to go and knock on Mrs X's door to ask if she is all right,' people say. 'She might resent it as an intrusion.' But a copy of *YOURS* in the hand is a bona fide reason for a call and the visitor may well be invited in, even if only to collect the 10p for the copy, which gives an opportunity for a chat and a quick assessment of how things are with the old person. There are between 7,000 and 8,000 volunteers doing this job. But isn't that, one asks, the form of grass-roots involvement which Age Concern has developed so well and for which it has so many experienced volunteers?

Age Concern has its own quarterly magazine, *New Age,* which appeals mainly to people involved in work for Age Concern and its offshoots, to sociologists and to social workers, both voluntary and professional. It deserves the journalist's accolade of 'a good read', being well written, well presented and very stimulating in the variety of its content. Where else, for instance, would most of us have read of the Grey Panthers of the USA and their remarkable leader, Maggie Kuhn? *New Age* and *YOURS* have a strong individuality and serve a different readership, but looking at the constant flow of pamphlets, information leaflets, reports, surveys and so forth coming out of all these organizations one is bound to wonder whether a joint publications and information service might be considered.

As for research, the CPA is funded as the major research organization, but Age Concern also goes in for research in a big way. In the first instance, as David Hobman explains, it needed to ask questions about what its policy and its chief activities should be, but is this still the case? It has its own research advisory group of distinguished people, with Dr Mark Abrams as its director (himself well past normal retiring age and a model of clarity and logic in his writings and speeches). Again, Help the Aged and Age Concern have both been concerned in sheltered housing, though both have encouraged the associations they have fostered to 'go it alone'. All the national organizations

155

also make representations to the Government and local authorities, not always jointly. All three appeal for financial support. Age Concern is the only one that gets Government aid, because it is the only one that normally provides personal service for the elderly on the ground.

You could say there was a sort of gentlemen's agreement between these three major organizations to co-operate and to concentrate on their own areas, but strong personalities and strong traditions are involved and they all prefer to do things in their own way and entirely under their own steam. Hugh Faulkner, in fact, says bluntly that people should not get together to do the same things but should try to be expert at their own job 'for the moment you say "let's co-operate" there is a tendency for the tempo to slacken. Better to be single-minded about what you think you should be doing and get on with it. If the other organizations do likewise, the total effect is greater.'

There is, though, an obvious need to keep battling on with forming an agreed policy and this concerns not only the voluntary and charitable organizations but the 'political' organizations, the campaigners, like Pensioners' Voice and especially the trade unions. In 1979 the Trades Union Congress brought together a wide spectrum of organizations concerned with the elderly, and many individuals who had seen notices in *YOURS* and other publications, in Central Hall, Westminster, at what they called a National Pensioners' Convention. And for the first time ever, the trade union organizations, the pensioners' associations and the charitable organizations agreed on a Declaration of Intent. It is as well that as many people of pensionable age as possible should know what is being campaigned for on their behalf, and what this or any subsequent Government is being asked to finance. The Declaration read:

This convention declares that every pensioner has the right to choice, dignity, independence and security as an integral and valued member of society. These rights require an adequate State retirement pension. There must be an immediate commitment to a pension level of not less than one half of average gross earnings for a married couple and not less than one-third of average gross earnings for a single person, upgraded at six-monthly intervals.

In addition to an adequate income a pensioner should, as of right:

Live in accommodation which is appropriate to personal need and circumstances with a reasonable degree of choice, including sheltered housing.

Be able to call on the full range of community and personal social services to give full support as need arises, including chiropody, television and telephone.

Be able to use a national scheme of substantial concessionary facilities on all public transport in all parts of the country.

Have ready access to comprehensive free health care on demand.

Be able to maintain a warm and well-lit home with adequate heating allowances covering all fuels.

Have full access to a varied and extensive range of education and leisure facilities.

Be paid a regular tax free Christmas bonus of £20, adjusted in future in line with inflation.

Be eligible for an adequate retirement pension on ceasing work at any time of his or her choice after the age of 60 years, without being subject to an earnings rule.

Be entitled to an adequate death grant regardless of age.

Among the Top Brass speaking in support of this Declaration, Len Murray, general secretary of the Trades Union Congress, was the weightiest and he spoke movingly and powerfully about the responsibility of trade unionists still at work to pay for better pensions for the retired, and benefits for the unemployed and the sick. But the financial burden implementation of the Declaration would impose is stiff. Mr Murray said, 'Figures of the order of £5,000 million have been quoted as the additional cost to the National Insurance Scheme of providing pensions of the order set.' If the Department of Health and Social Security estimates quoted above (p. 139) are correct, it would mean adding something like 50 per cent to the present cost of caring for the elderly. Of this Mr Murray said, 'The problem is not whether we can afford to pay these amounts, but *how* these amounts will be raised.'

It is true that the new industrial pension schemes safeguard the future for most employed persons under the age of forty-five. But what is going to happen in the next eighteen years or so? Conservative Government intentions to make 'public spending cuts' in the 1980s quickly caused alarm in pensioners' organizations. Pension rises were tied to price rises from 1973, but as part of the social contract between the Labour Government and the trade unions in 1974, not only was there a substantial increase in the retirement pension, but it was laid down that there should be an annual review to ensure that the pension was increased to match the increase either in wage rates or

158

in prices, whichever was the greater. In the autumn of 1979 the Conservative Government abolished the automatic link with rises in wages, maintaining only the link with prices. In the then economic climate it was not surprising that fears were voiced that the annual pension review might also be ended.

Have the working population in general and trade unionists in particular really accepted that a commitment to pay pensions of up to half of national average earnings means a readiness to pay higher national insurance contributions, increased income tax, or increased VAT? Jack Jones, one of the most influential voices in the trade union movement added his word to Len Murray's in a conversation I had with him. 'Higher national insurance contributions might help to meet the cost of increased pensions. I don't think we should shudder at the idea of increased income tax if it is going to meet the needs of the old people — on the principle that this is an absolute priority. You can't run a nation like this without having income from the people, and income tax is the best way of ensuring that everybody makes a contribution.'

But he went on to say, as do so many trade unionists and Labour supporters: 'If you ask me, I think that there are lots and lots of economies that can be made and the greatest economy we should be striving for is to find ways of reducing the arms race.' 'Having your cake and eating it', economics are common to all parties. The Labour view that slashing the defence budget would automatically provide the Exchequer with ample funds to take care of the needs of the aged is not more fanciful than the Conservative view that 'cuts in public spending' will automatically put the economy in good heart. Where to put the emphasis in getting and spending is really what politics is all about.

The pensioners' Declaration itself involved more compromises than might be obvious at first sight. There is, for example, a strong feeling that all efforts should be concentrated on raising pensions to the level at which retired people can afford full choice and do not need to depend on hand-outs. Many trade unionists hold this view and resent having hand-outs with the smell of charity about them. Age Concern's David Hobman admits that he, too, is personally 'four-square against vouchers of any kind', and regards them as a very bad alternative to real income. But when Age Concern did a survey of pensioners' attitudes towards concessionary travel, he realized that most didn't see how in their lifetime they were going to have an adequate income, so that concessionary travel was welcome. Jack Jones, who is now a vigorous spokesman for the Transport and General Workers Union's 'Retired Members' Association', gives free travel top priority amongst his own aims.

He gave the Pensioners' Convention some shaming information about the anomalies in the provision of concessionary travel. In Greater London all pensioners can have bus passes entitling them to *free* travel outside rush hours; the pass also applies to travel on the Underground in off-peak hours (a 20p ticket will take the pensioner from one end of the network to another, even if the normal fare is £2 or so). Over the country a total of 2,250,000 pensioners are estimated to enjoy free bus travel and 5,000,000 have a half-fare concession. But, said Mr Jones, there are nearly fifty non-metropolitan districts which have *no* concessionary travel scheme. No fewer than 800,000 pensioners are estimated to live in areas without travel concessions.

Here Jack Jones's thinking is more in line with his members', I imagine, than David Hobman's. If you give elderly people an extra 50p a week on the pension, hoping they will spend it on getting out and about, most of them *won't*. But give them a travel pass and they will almost certainly use it, to the great benefit of their health and spirits. As Jack Jones puts it, 'The more you provide free travel and good community centres, the less there will be people who have to go into hospital.' And surely it is important to remember that a concession like a free bus pass is inflation proof, unlike cash pensions and some other benefits. What about the Christmas bonus? It has halved in value since it was introduced in 1973. As for the death grant, much more important to people of retirement age than to younger people, it is estimated to have been reduced in value by 500 per cent. Fixed at £20 when it was introduced in 1949 and increased to £30 in 1967, it is ludicrously inadequate today. Even if the increase to £125 proposed by an all-party group of MPs, the 'Death With Dignity' group, were accepted by the Government, it would be nowhere near enough to cover funeral costs today.

I myself believe that it would be a more certain protection of the very old and frail against hypothermia to make available vouchers usable for any kind of fuel -- electricity, gas, oil, coal, coke, or even paraffin -- than to raise the pension by some smallish sum, or to assume that all who live in damp, draughty homes or who suffer from rheumatism, arthritis, bronchitis or any crippling illness will apply for supplementary benefit to help them to pay for extra heating. They did not apply for the grant for insulating their homes in anything like the expected numbers. 'Choice' sounds fine, but so often it turns out to mean *asking* for help, which many elderly people inevitably think of as asking for charity. Far too many pensioners fail to claim supplementary benefits, rent rebates and so on – because they think it is 'undignified', 'humiliating' or what 'lazy lay-abouts and scroungers do', not thrifty, hard-working citizens like them.

Choice of fuel, though, should not be ignored by housing authorities. George Dunn of the National Federation of Old Age Pension Associations, is one of the people who think that there is a strong argument for retaining the 'outmoded' fireplace and flue. He argues that our present technological society tends to take away choice from the elderly and confront them with appliances which they do not want and do not always understand. Certainly, panel and under-floor heating and night storage heaters have turned out to be much more costly in operation than we were told. Solid fuel has drawbacks – it is heavy to carry from cellar or coal bunker to fireplace; it makes much work in cleaning the grate and adds much dust and grime in the home, but it has two real advantages: the blazing hearth is like a welcoming friend in the house, and weekly or monthly fuel expenditure is much easier to calculate if one has to pay the coalman for each bag delivered than if one has to work out how many therms of gas or units of electricity each appliance is using per hour. It is almost certain that many very old people are scared of using their gas or electric heaters as often as they ought for comfort or even for safety. Isn't this a very strong agrument for some kind of a fuel voucher, at least on the recommendation of a GP, even if not for all people of a certain age? Younger people are probably not fully aware of how frightening inflation is to old people and what a psychological effect it has on their spending. If for most of your adult life you have thought of a rubber hot water bottle, for example, as costing not more than 30p and you find that it now costs over £2, you don't, like a younger person, grumble and pay up. You do without.

There is one policy conflict over provision for the ageing which is too deep and serious to be papered over and which needs a great deal more research and honest and open-minded discussion between all age groups than it has had: the question of whether mandatory retirement is a desirable thing, and if so, at what age. The 1979 Pensioners' Convention laid it down that everyone 'should be eligible for an adequate retirement pension on leaving work at any time of his or her choice after the age of 60 years, without being subject to an earnings rule'. Age Concern's policy document (Clause 112) says, 'We believe that plans should be prepared now for introducing a flexible retirement system over the next ten years, identifying a wide band to be used as a retirement period.' Help the Aged takes a similar line. Yet trade union policy has traditionally been to press for a reduced retirement age, and the 1979 Trades Union Congress spelled it out in a resolution which read: 'Congress calls upon the TUC and Labour movement to take every form of action to compel the Government to reduce the pensionable age to 60, if necessary by stages. Congress also calls upon the Government to introduce the necessary changes in Social Security legislation so that there is provision whereby any person retiring early under the provision of a statutory or industrial scheme shall be able to qualify immediately for the State retirement pension.'

This resolution stood in the names of the National

Union of Mineworkers and the Constructional section of the Amalgamated Union of Engineering Workers. It was supported by three white collar unions, the Transport Salaried Staffs Association, the Society of Post Office Executives and the National Union of Teachers. Whenever 'pension age' comes up in any discussion one is quickly made aware that orthodox trade unionists tend to assume 'the earlier the better'. It is interesting that when men say the age differential between men and women is unfair they mean that retirement at sixty-five for men, sixty for women, is unfair to men. When women say it is unfair quite a lot of them mean that it is unfair to women — though young feminists often need to be reminded that not all older women see compulsory retirement on pension at sixty as a boon to be cherished at all costs.

Trade union delegates should also be reminded that those who are concerned for the welfare of the retired, as distinct from the still employed, are almost all committed to flexibility for everyone able and fit for work. Hugh Faulkner of Help the Aged says quite bluntly, 'Despite fine-sounding statements about opportunities to stay on in employment, more and more of the elderly have been excluded from employment in the last 30 years. Retirement has rapidly become associated in this country with fixed pension ages, irrespective of individual variations in health and capacity. An increasing number of people wish to go on working in some useful, worthwhile capacity.'

David Hobman, advocating flexible retirement within a band of ten years or so, is outspoken about trade union hostility to the idea. 'When it comes to the crunch, I suspect they really *want* to see the old men off.' And Hugh Faulkner again: 'I think it is terribly important that people shouldn't be faced

164

with the situation that, come 60 or 65, CHOP! Now you are a different person and will have to manage on a pension of £x!' There is a not unjustified feeling that the older trade union leaders who have spent their lives negotiating for higher wages and shorter hours see their function only in those terms.

It is seldom remembered now that the pension age originally, in 1905, was seventy, for both sexes. Health care and nutrition being far less adequate then than now, the years between sixty and seventy were a miserable struggle for many. Trade union memories are long — that may be the main reason why there has always been a drive to reduce the pension age. In 1928 it became possible for both sexes to claim a pension at sixty-five. Why did the wartime Government decide in 1940 to lower the pension age for women to sixty? It was mainly for the sake of wives who couldn't draw a pension until they were sixty-five, even though their husbands were as much as ten years older, which was by no means uncommon. Ten years of life for two on one pension was pretty hard, and letting the woman have her pension five years earlier saved the Exchequer the cost of paying double pensions to married couples immediately the husband reached sixty-five. There was also lingering sympathy for the 'spinster' who had been so unlucky as to fail to find a husband to maintain her (many of this generation's potential husbands had been killed in the First World War) and probably had to care for one or both frail, elderly parents.

In 1948 the chief reason for the earlier pension for women was removed, when the married man became entitled to a 'dependency benefit' for his wife — but the nettle of equalizing the pension age was again not grasped and remains a source of grievance to many people. When the pension differential was discussed in the House of Commons in 1975, the then Minister for Social Security, Barbara Castle, suggested that 'the lower retirement age for women is some compensation to them for the lower wages they have been drawing all these years, when women have been exploited and paid merely sweated wages'. It seems to me an odd compensation for low wages to say, 'You can go on pension now which is a good deal less even than your sweated wages and only about 25 per cent of what your male colleagues will continue to be able to earn for the next five years.' But Barbara Castle's view reflected exactly the commonly held trade union view that moving from a wage or salary to a pension is a boon to be grasped with two eager hands.

What the trade unions might well concentrate on now is the total abolition of the detested 'earnings rule'. Constant agitation has persuaded past Governments to raise the amount which people can earn without deduction from their pension, but until men, married couples and single women stand on the same terms as widows, who for many years have had the right to earn without deduction, there will be resentment.

While the statisticians work out the economics of earlier retirement for men or later retirement for women, to equalize the pension age or debate the feasibility of flexible retirement, most organizations concerned with the care of the elderly know that there is a condition called 'retirement shock' and an even more prevalent and serious condition which one can describe as a gradual paralysis of the responses, which tends to start when there is no commitment to a job. There is also, some economists admit, an effect called 'retirement blight' which limits a person's prospects of promotion in his or her fifties. An Age Concern discussion document *Ageing in the 80s* said that firms which elect to pay retirement pensions linked to seniority, or who are obliged to pay retirement pensions, are unwilling to take on men in their fifties.

Questioned directly about the pension age, trade union leaders are quick to explain that what they are talking about is the age at which the national state pension is payable, and not compulsory retirement. If you say, as I said to Jack Jones, that you fear that a *permissible* age of retirement may become the *compulsory* age, you are likely to be told that 'compulsion' comes from the employers who get rid of employees at sixty-five, sixty or even younger, when they want to reduce the work force. 'The idea that the trade unions are all powerful and the employers have no powers is just nonsense. Employees soon discover that if there is a reduction in trade or a rationalization in industry, or if new technologies are introduced, employers will just sack them. They may now, when the trade union movement is stronger than it used to be, make lump sum severance payments, but these are just a momentary help, and of no long term consequence.'

Mr Jones thinks that to some extent we do operate a flexible retirement system here, but he poured cold water on the idea that it would be possible to introduce a law which could force employers to retain on their books old people who wanted to stay at work. When I cited the success of Maggie Kuhn and her Grey Panthers in outlawing the compulsory retirement of federal employees he said, 'I doubt if that provision will make much impact on the population at large. All it really means is that in the odd case where a person wants to continue to work in the public service he will be allowed to do so. Well, that's OK for the US.'

But Maggie Kuhn's driving force should be better understood by trade unionists here. When she was compulsorily retired from her social welfare job she felt, she said, that she was losing 'the most important identity-forming role in our society', her job. 'Our throwaway society, with its matching throwaway mentality, scrap-piles people as it does automobiles,' she argues. Her view *vis-à-vis* the British trade unions is that they should be 're-cycling people'. We re-cycle paper, water, even industrial waste,' says this vivacious, energetic leader of 15,000 campaigners, who not only travels continually across Northern America but has been several times to Great Britain, has appeared on British television and has been interviewed for articles in newspapers and journals all over the place.

It is significant, though, that the Trades Union Congress 1979 resolution on retirement stood in the name not only of the miners and constructional engineers but also of the teachers. This reveals an important truth, that people in stress occupations, of which teaching tends to be one, as well as the people in heavy and dangerous jobs, often regard retirement as a boon. Jack Jones had no doubt at all that a huge majority of the Transport and General Workers Union members would opt for earlier retirement, given the choice and given 'a good solid pension' – and he regards boosting the pension as the union's most important current task. 'If you leave the age of 65 for the state pension for the moment and get the pension right, then you make it possible to take the next step later on.' But this argument, which appears to give the employee a true right of choice, to work or not to work, seems to me simplistic, both in economic and in psychological terms.

In favour of early retirement there is the need, the argument goes, to save the country the cost of paying unemployment benefit to great numbers of young workers, and risking their being jobless so long that they may become unemployable. But on the other hand the cost is immense of providing pensions for non-productive citizens, more and more of whom, inconveniently for the economy, are living longer and longer. These ageing and aged people can only be maintained by the current labour force, through taxes and insurance contributions, and the burden threatens to become very heavy. In 1948 five working people supported one pensioned person. In 1978, 3.5 working people supported one pensioned person. It has been said that at General Motors, in the USA, there were ten workers in 1967 for every company pensioner; by 1979 there were only four; and in the 1990s there is expected to be only one. It is true that one worker may, through new technology, be so productive by 1990 that his labours will easily support several pensioners as well as his own family, and of course the pensioner himself will have contributed substantially through his social security payments to his pension and will continue to pay income tax on it.

But has the economic equation been convincingly worked out? And can we ever afford to treat human beings as symbols on paper or dots on a graph? The temptation, even in this decade, is to regard married women as only 'pin-money' or at best 'supplementary' workers and to accept that men's need of paid employment is always and for ever greater than their own. The same attitude seems to pertain towards older people of both sexes. The young, starting out in life,

169

the middle-aged with families to maintain, need the jobs in a way the old do not, it is assumed. To me flexible retirement, at any age between, say, sixty and seventy (with a special option of fifty-five for workers in dangerous jobs) seems a basic human right. It would enable male and female workers to be treated equally and the different needs, temperaments, mental and physical attributes, life experience and life expectancy of all wage and salary workers to be acknowledged and catered for. Not everyone thinks that could be easily achieved. David Hobman of Age Concern admits that it might be 'more judgmental' than mandatory retirement; someone has to decide whether the man of seventy should or should not retire, if he does not wish to — and one can imagine that the appeals procedure involved with such decisions might seem as harsh as means-testing for the 'dole' used to be.

There is some evidence from the United States that it is possible for industrial companies to operate a 'free' retirement policy, as well as the public service. Bankers Life and Casualty Company of Chicago, a very large insurance company, has had no compulsory retirement for the last forty years. The practice was introduced by the then president of the company when he was only forty years old. He believed that older workers have unique skills, and the company not only retains older employees but hires new staff over sixty-five if they have the ability to do the job. The company's policy evidently works, for it is able to report 'major growth'. Difficulties which could arise through younger employees' promotion being blocked, or older employees finding their jobs getting on top of them are ironed out by employment counselling and job training.

Another large insurance company, Connecticut

General Life, with 13,000 employees, eliminated mandatory retirement in 1977, 'except for its 1000 officers and field managers'. These employees may also continue to work if they accept lesser job responsibility. This seems to be a developing pattern in the USA. US Steel employ 15,000 workers who 'usually retire after thirty years' employment'. For those not ready to retire, the company and union may consult together and find physically less demanding jobs. Such jobs, apparently, are plentiful, and the productivity of the older workers is thought to be greater than that of the younger employees.

There is another economic problem which has never been sorted out. If the sixty-year-old retires because he/she is exhausted by the physical or psychological demands of the job, is it equitable that he/she should be entitled only to a lower pension than the person who continues to receive a good income for working at a job he/she enjoys until the age of sixty-five? Are reduced pensions for early retirement desirable? Do they work as an inducement, or a compensation? In simple terms, the question seems to be, 'Do you reward a person who stays at work and contributes to the economy by a larger pension, or do you bribe, with cash bonuses or some form of "redundancy pay" the person who takes himself/herself out of the labour force early?'

What hard evidence is there of the wishes of the majority of the workers themselves *both before and after retirement?* (Asking the question, 'Do you wish to retire at 60?' surely needs to be checked later with the question, 'Are you glad you retired at 60?') Has anyone done a comprehensive survey of the practice of the self-employed, who can please themselves? Journalists, authors, actors, musicians, lawyers, doctors and many other professional people are able to continue to exercise their skills, and most do so. But what about shopkeepers and other small businessmen? Newsagents and the proprietors of fish and chip shops are commonly supposed to make a lot of money in a very few years by working extremely hard at unsocial hours and then to retire to the Costa Geriatrica or going on a series of world cruises, but this is probably an exaggeration and not likely to be at all typical of other independent earners. Do plumbers, boot repairers, electricians, corner shop and boutique owners down tools the moment they become eligible for the pension? Has anyone ever done a survey of them?

It is too easy to make assumptions about the wishes of the 'retired' themselves. Chris Phillipson, writing as director of the pre-retirement education research project at Keele University, asserted that the fear of retirement is greatly exaggerated. 'If you discount those whose fears are centred round the drop in income, the fears are probably very small.' Get the pension right, as Jack Jones and other trade union leaders would say, and all will be perfect. That itself is going to take a long time. Even the most energetic trade union campaigners are only asking for a third of the national average earnings for a single pensioner and half for a married couple. Half pay is half pay — not very agreeable, even if you get it without 'the daily grind'. But do healthy, energetic adults really want to live for years on a hand-out, whether you call it a 'dole' or a 'pension'? Some do; others certainly don't.

But the problem of 'redundancy' has now to be seen as part of a problem facing the whole Western world. The new Industrial Revolution, the age of micro-electronics, of the silicon chip, is upon us. There is no doubt at all that by the turn of this century far fewer employees will be needed to provide us with goods and services and that they will be needed for far fewer hours per day or days per week. In the last fifteen years, 2,500,000 jobs had disappeared because of containerization in the docks, mechanization of the mines and the introduction of automation in the engineering industry. Even in agriculture it is estimated that about 600,000 jobs have gone because of mechanization. Mechanization may be a very good thing, but it is very largely responsible for the fact that in the United Kingdom, at the time of writing, there are verging on 2,000,000 unemployed.

To stand up and say, 'You must not deny a man employment when he reaches a certain age' may be as Luddite as to say, 'You must not use this new machine.' Calls for earlier retirement, heard increasingly often as the unemployment figures mount, like calls for shorter working hours, have to be examined in new terms. How are we to make a satisfactory pattern of lives in which so much less time is spent at work? We should never forget Isaac Watts's adage, 'Satan finds some mischief still for idle hands to do.' A bored person is a person at risk, whether he is sixteen or sixty. The youngster may take to vandalism and punch-ups. The old person may sag into apathy and chronic ill-health. We have not got very far yet. The suggestion of people like Keele's Chris Phillipson tend to be for increased financial resources, such as part of the revenue from North Sea oil, 'to provide a network of communal facilities for retired people', or 'a special tax to be levied on all firms with more than 250 employees, the proceeds going to the provision of additional health and welfare facilities to rural areas and regions with a high concentration of elderly people.' The most patronizing suggestion of all is that the unemployed, especially teachers and building workers, could provide 'a valuable service to the elderly', the former running educational courses for the retired and the latter doing repair work inside their homes. (How many of these compulsorily retired men and women could show the unemployed youngsters a thing or two, and would be glad to be recruited to do so?)

More worth looking at are schemes being tried out, especially in America, of increasing the time spent away from work. One plan is to increase gradually the length of the annual vacation after the age of, say, fifty-five; another is to shorten the working day gradually. Some industries are already moving towards a four-day working week and regular three-day weekends. This kind of work pattern would force us all to find ways of using 'large blocks of leisure time'. Some American firms are experimenting with reducing pay for extended holidays in the five years preceding retirement, with the aim of getting the worker used to managing on a 'retirement income'.

Such experiments are no more than tentative nibbles at the colossal problem of getting us used to the idea of *not* working. Somehow we have to shed the concept of 'enough jobs to go round', which leads to attempts to take whole sections of the population out of the job market — keeping children at school or college longer; telling wives they can be more usefully occupied at home; expecting the sixty-plus people to entertain themselves at Darby and Joan Clubs or 'pop-in parlours'.

Surely more bracing than the framework of Age Concern or Help the Aged, so far as retired people themselves are concerned, is the framework of the

American National Council of Senior Citizens. It started out in 1961 to fight for the passage of Medicare — and this, it is important to note, was not solely to benefit senior citizens: 'We saw how hard we had to fight for the right to Medicare, which freed the middle-aged from the double burden of educating their children and providing medical care for their parents.' And this led the founders to believe that they could 'mobilize the elderly behind progressive programmes that would help to provide a better life for all Americans, old and young.' The watchword of the National Council of Senior Citizens is: 'Although many of us are retired from our jobs we are not retired from citizenship.'

This tonic emphasis on the importance of the participation of the elderly in running the country *for the benefit of all* prompts another thought. We are all in the microchip revolution together. Perhaps while management and unions battle with the practicalities of operation the new technology, the people who already have experience of living without paid employment could most usefully share their ideas on introducing new concepts of daily living. Retired persons who have seen the line blur between the work you do for money and the work you do because you want to, have perhaps more to offer than at any other time in their lives. That the pursuits you *choose* impose their own discipline, their own orderly pattern on your life is what all happily retired people would like to communicate. That we can and should continue to be involved in 'politics' in the widest sense, as long as we live, is what we ought to be telling the world.

8
Doorway

WE are not old. As Bernard Baruch is reported to have said, 'Old is always fifteen years older than I am.' We are young to ourselves most of our lives, young to our elders as long as we have any. A friend of eighty-one, knowing from her son of the way I over-filled my sixties with activities, said fondly, 'What it is to be young!' Perhaps by seventy one is finding, disconcertingly, that people express no surprise when one says, 'Of course, I'm getting old.' There may come a day, in our late eighties perhaps, when we shall actually brag about our age. I don't know about that yet. 'Old' is fifteen years older than I am.

We who have reached and passed the allotted span have, of course, *something* to brag about. A survey that Dr Mark Abrams conducted for Age Concern in 1978 showed that of all the babies born in Britain at the beginning of the twentieth century, almost a third had died by 1946 — many as a result of two world wars — and another 40 per cent by 1977. Only 30 per cent of the turn-of-the-century babies were still alive. They were the *survivors*, and they have a right to be boastful, if life is still good for them, of the health, energy and will-power that have kept them going longer than their contemporaries who came into the world with the same life expectancy. But in the eighth decade, in this 'borrowed time', even if not earlier, there are plain intimations of mortality, clear evidence in the way our body fails to respond so punctiliously to the brain's commands that it is obviously not what it was, that it is now coming slowly and not frighteningly to the end of its ability to function.

It is our late autumn; it is our early winter. Outside my window as I write, in a very mild December, there are nasturtiums, still luxuriantly green, with a few small orange flowers. But their time has gone by. The dahlias were black on their stems a couple of weeks ago; there are still a few roses, but their petals fall almost as soon as they are brought indoors. For some of us winter comes as late as it has to this year's nasturtiums, but come it will, and not very many of us over-seventies will see the end of the decade that has just begun.

Throughout our sixties most of us push out of our minds the thought that death is coming quite close, despite the funerals of contemporaries, despite the fact that the Christmas card list shrinks each year. The day approaches when *our* names will be crossed out of address books. Is it not time to drag this thought out of its hiding place and have a good look at it? Self-deception is the most shameful of human weaknesses. There is no way to cheat death. In Schubert's *Death and the Maiden* the German words read: *Bin Freund und komme nicht zu strafen* ('I come as friend, not foe'). In our true old age we enter into the post-lude, our *real*, not enforced, retirement. If our muscles seize up, or if we are afflicted with arthritis, we may be immobilized. If our sight fails, we shall not be able to read. If our hearing goes, we shall not be able to converse or listen to radio or TV. If our memory goes, we tend to think, all goes.

So we fight or we give in. How long, how hard, do we fight our increasing disabilities? How soon do we accept them? Fighting is best, I think, for as long as we can — the cataract operation, the stronger and stronger lenses and magnifying glasses, the large-print books, the discreet hearing aids, the gradual increase in visual rather than aural communication, the aids to mobility, the walking sticks, walking frames, wheel chairs. But how to combat that humiliating memory loss? Most importantly, I believe, by accepting that it is fundamentally a *physical* affliction, to do with the supply of blood to the brain cells, for this puts it on a par with muscular failure rather than feebleness of the mind and will. Writing everything down immediately may be the best help — addresses, telephone numbers, significant items heard on radio or TV or read in newspapers and books. A friend afflicted in this way and worrying incessantly about her memory failure said, 'I feel I have lost the top layer of my brain, and I am so afraid that my friends will think that I am not interested in their affairs if I forget to comment on their letters or their doings.'

Memory failures are odd and disconcerting. It is as if the points of the brain's traffic system get stuck or switched, so that the thought processes are halted or get onto the wrong track. For most people the best plan, when a name or a word fails to arrive, is to say, 'Never mind. It will come in a moment' — and it usually does if one doesn't fuss. Some of us are verbally more visual than aural, and with us it helps to write everything down. Mnemonics are a help, even jingles of the kind we learned at school to fix in our minds the kings of England or Latin genders or conjugations. We can all invent our own ingenious tricks. It is much easier for me to remember a phone number if I say aloud, for instance, 'Twenty-two and ninepence' for 2209.

Why certain words *always* vanish when wanted is an interesting mystery. Perhaps one ought to practise exercises in synonyms, as we practise finger-flexing or knee-bending, holding onto the towel rail? I discovered that I could remember *one* of two pairs of words but never the other. If I could remember jacaranda, I could not remember agapanthus and vice versa. If I could remember Citroen, I could not remember Renault. Friends laughed unsympathetically, asking how often I would need to use any of these words. But I battled on, for it wasn't the words I needed; it was the need to be able to produce any word instantly. And I won.

All my memory-jogging techniques once failed to produce the surname of a friend who sent a Christmas card signed only 'Grace', but Alex Comfort's suggestion is worth trying — to go through the alphabet until you strike a letter which rings a bell, then through the vowels until you get a syllable and so on. But he emphasizes, in his bracing fashion, that the best way of improving memory and all other mental perform-ance is to use your faculties through continued activity, learning and 'enrichment of the environment'. Mental deterioration, he asserts, 'would occur at any age if we only had a television set'.

But in the long run we are not going to win our battles. Sir Robert Mayer, at 100, on the much-loved TV programme *Face the Music*, forgot the name of the Brahms work he had hoped to play when he actually met Brahms. You wouldn't think it possible that, even after the better part of a century, he could forget such an important fact. But he did, and so shall we, more and more often. So should we not be pre-paring ourselves, consciously though without fuss, to cede defeat? Should we not be thinking soon about retrenching, discarding, shedding, withdrawing? This can be quite important in the literal, physical sense. As we 'brought nothing into this world', it is certain that 'we carry nothing out', and what is more, we are probably not going to be able to carry along with us right to the very end all the things we have acquired over the years. So many books we are never going to read again, so much music we shan't play or sing; so much china, silver and glass that is surplus to requirements. Why do we hang on to it all? Out of habit, because we have always had a home filled with possessions that reflected our way of life? To give us the feeling that life goes on as it always has? Or just out of apathy? Not long ago I was summoned, with two friends to the Buckinghamshire home of Lady (Gertrude) Williams, formerly Professor of Social Economics at Bedford College, University of London, to choose as many books as we wished for the Fawcett Library, that remarkable repository of books by, about and for women now housed at the City of London Polytechnic. Lady Williams had already given away at least 2,000 volumes to colleges and institutions of higher education, especially those short of funds because of lack of endowments or budgetary cuts. To shed one's possessions in this way is a positive affirmation, not a dispirited retreat. It also can win affection and admiration, which are welcome at any time, especially in lonely old age.

Whether we are able to live right to the end in our own home or move to some kind of 'sheltered' accommodation, too many possessions will be a problem in our great old age. Some women find great satisfaction, right to the end of their lives, in cleaning, dusting and polishing, but as energy and determination lessen and inertia creeps in, the cleaning and tidying chores tend to be put off and off and off, and the home gradually becomes untended, unkempt and even positively dirty. Not *ours*? No, of course not. But will-power sags, especially in those who have lost their lifetime partner, as most of the very old have, especially women. According to Dr Abrams's survey *Beyond Three-Score-and-Ten*, 79 per cent of men between the ages of sixty-five and seventy-four still have the company of a wife, but 34 per cent of women are already widowed. After the age of seventy-five the number of men with a wife still living has dropped to 67 per cent and of women with a husband, to a pitiful 18 per cent. Couples are loth to shed their goods lest either should deprive or hurt the feelings of the other, but the widow and the widower are liable to look around the home and say sadly or bitterly, 'All this just for me? It's too much.'

To go into any kind of new home, even a well-equipped local authority flatlet, means a great shedding of possessions. I pruned once, after my husband died, drastically and painfully. It could not, surely, be as searing a second time. Kind, concerned people think that the older one grows, the more one clings to possessions. I greatly doubt if this is true for more than a few. One's hold on material goods tends to slacken even before one's hold on life noticeably slackens. It will have to slacken even further if, in the last period, 'home' is a geriatric ward or a nursing unit. Isn't it as well to think from time to time which are the things that really matter? Many people, especially women, find cataloguing and indexing their effects quite an interesting and rewarding occupation and positively enjoy leaving instructions: 'My ruby ring to my niece Esther; my sherry glasses and decanter to my nephew Timothy' and so on. Not so many men do this, being less close to their domestic possessions, perhaps, but some loving husbands and fathers prepare in another way, by leaving clear directions about what needs to be done, and when, and how, by the person who will be in charge when he dies. No deed could be kinder or less morbid and sentimental.

However or whenever it is done, the shedding or allocating of possessions is essentially a statement that in our great age we shall not need them, nor be able to look after them nor, in all probability, have room for them. It is accepting Teilhard de Chardin's concept of 'diminishment'. And I think one has to learn to see this as affecting our powers as well as our possessions.

Does this sound a bleak prospect, especially if it entails the need to be nursed and tended day by day? Perhaps — yet at this time isn't one beginning to drift away from material surroundings and find value almost solely in human contacts? A chaplain I talked to at a south-east London residential estate for retired people had no doubt that the nursing unit there was an immense blessing. The charity had built the forty-bed special unit to serve the community of 230, which meant that the very old, the sick and the frail could continue to be cherished by a staff they knew and trusted and to be visited by good friends among the residents. 'Some people', said the chaplain, 'would say it is sad having what they call a "death house" in the grounds, but in my experience those who have been to hospital for an operation and come back, and those who in the end have moved to this unit, have been very grateful for it. They hated the idea of being sent off to a geriatric ward and dying in a strange hospital. The continuity and familiarity of the place have been extremely precious to them.'

At this point we are all confronted with the fact that dying, our dying, may be wretched, lonely, undignified, perhaps extremely painful. So what can be done about it, for our sake and all others in their turn? There is a strong movement among the housing associations and charitable trusts to provide special units within their own framework where the terminally ill can be nursed. There is a vigorous growth of the hospice movement, made widely known through the work of Dame Cicely Saunders at St Christopher's Hospice in Surbiton, and St Joseph's Hospice, Hackney, about which an *Everyman* television programme was made and shown one Sunday night. A symposium in 1979 at the Brook General Hospital in south-east London was told of widespread development of the hospice movment and, in particular, of plans for smallish units, not necessarily run by religious communities, in Oxford, Manchester, Lincoln, Leeds, Glasgow and Edinburgh. Dame Cicely estimated at the beginning of 1980 that there were no fewer than fifty hospices about the country. It seems established that in these hospices pain, even the very severe pain caused by some terminal cancers, can almost always be controlled. (There is a minority of cases where even here pain control fails.) The medical director of St Joseph's said on the TV programme that about 60 per cent of the patients had pain of varying sorts, and that in terminal illness it is 'constant, over-whelming pain which colours the patient's whole mentality. Such patients can't concentrate, can't think. It affects their social activities. They don't want to do anything, they don't want to talk. They want, as it were, to hide their heads under the pillow.'

That is the kind of description that makes every normal person *afraid* of dying. But, said the St Joseph's doctor, 'This is the kind of pain we can do something about. The method is to use the opium-based drugs earlier rather than later, enough at a time and at regular intervals, always before the effect of the previous dose has worn off. We keep the drug at a sufficient level to erase the patient's pain altogether.' Enough is known now about the control of the agonizing pain associated with cancer to make it the *right* of a sufferer to be given relief. Doesn't it seem unlikely that pain control of this kind can only be safely administered and achieved in the hospices where a special study has been made of it? They usually operate on a basis of one nurse per hospital bed — an impossible ratio to maintain all over the country. So one constantly hears of distressing cases of long-drawn-out misery, if not worse. Over-drugging is quite often mentioned, too, especially by a loving son, daughter or spouse, who is convinced that communication has been established with the dying person and should not be blurred by a routine administration of pain-killers.

Helen Franks described such a moment in the last hours of her mother-in-law's life in a moving article in the *Guardian*. 'Her blue eyes, which had been heavy-lidded and half-closed with boredom for years, opened wide and clear and beautiful. "What am I doing here?" they were saying.' Helen Franks believed that by the action of the nurses she was deprived of a last precious moment of communication with a dear friend. Who was right, nurse or daughter-in-law? The patient herself was unable to say whether that moment of communication could be worth the pain it might have cost, or whether a pain-free, totally unconscious exit was preferable. A *Guardian* reader commenting on this article said that on the last day of her mother's life she rebelled against the doctor's order to give the patient 'a certain strong sleep-inducing pill.' The result, she declared, was that she and her mother were still in communication, frail as it might be, within seconds of her death. This daughter admitted that she didn't know whether she was right or not. No one can know.

But have we not all the right to some choice in the manner of our dying, apart from sudden death by accident or heart failure? A personal letter to me, written about the time of this article, told the story of a woman of eighty-nine who had suffered a paralysing attack which resulted in a coma. 'She was rushed to hospital and spent the next two years propped up in bed. Her bewildered and unhappy relatives had to travel many miles to visit her, although she was quite unable to recognize or communicate with them. They were not young themselves.' This writer described also the prolongation of lives without meaning which she had seen in her visits to geriatric hospitals.

Some are blind, stone-deaf, paralysed, painfully arthritic, mentally senile, 'sans everything' that makes life worth living. But they are resuscitated from heart attacks or strokes, forced to endure major surgery and amputations and to go on pointlessly through time. It was my misfortune to attend a lecture given by a docter in charge of one of these institutions. A smiling, urbane man in middle age, he stated that he had always had about one hundred senile, demented, incontinent old ladies in his care, and directly one of them seemed to be dying he rushed in with every resource possible to prevent it. Some of the audience, much shaken, demanded to know what for. But this was disregarded.

This picture of the medical 'technician', carried away by his own skill in maintaining the semblance of life when the reality has gone, is probably quite untypical of the profession. I am certain there is a widespread revulsion against 'artificial' means of keeping hearts just beating and lungs just inflating in bodies in which the brain has almost stopped functioning. The Archbishop of Cardiff, Dr John Murphy, probably spoke for almost all Christians, including Roman Catholics like himself, when he said on a Radio Wales programme in which I took part: 'I don't tolerate, I can't stand, extraordinary methods of keeping people alive. Anyone has a right to refuse an operation — if they are able. There is no good keeping cabbages alive by some sort of mechanical means. It is an abuse of the doctors' oath.'

I am convinced that it is reports of cases of these two kinds — the terribly painful terminal illness, and the condition in which the death of the mind and its ability to control the body's functions precedes the death of the body — that have produced the increased interest in the last few years in voluntary euthanasia. Opinion polls taken for EXIT (formerly the Voluntary Euthanasia Society) have consistently shown a majority in favour of voluntary euthanasia ever since 1938, though the majority has fluctuated from 62 per cent (1938 and 1979) to 69 per cent (1976) and only 55 per cent in 1950. (It is thought that the Nazis' use of the word 'euthanasia' for getting rid of millions of human beings whom they regarded as undesirable, on racial or any other grounds, affected this particular poll and probably gave many people a permanent revulsion against the whole concept of artificially induced death.)

The question asked by National Opinion Polls in

1979 which received an impressive 62 per cent 'Yes' answer was: 'Do you agree that if a patient is suffering from a distressing and incurable illness, a doctor should be allowed to supply that patient with the means to end his life, if the patient wishes to?' Active support for the society was certainly growing at that time — membership was then increasing at the rate of forty a month. The principal aim of EXIT is to secure the legal right of an adult person, suffering from a severe illness for which no relief is known, to receive an immediate death if, and only if, that is the person's expressed wish. The last time such a Bill came before Parliament was in 1969. Since then the atmosphere has changed notably. 'Mercy killings' are not infrequently reported, and judges are generally sympathetic towards the men or women in the dock who have given a beloved parent or spouse release. International co-operation is evident; each country learns from the others. It may be that it is still too early to expect a change in the law, but I have no doubt at all that it is on its way.

There are three kinds of objection to voluntary euthanasia. First, the religious. If you believe that God gave use life and only God should take it away, there can be no argument. Non-believers can only say that Christians must be prepared to accept that God's will, in their interpretation, may involve desperate suffering, not only for themselves but also for those they love most. The Christian view used to be that the greater the suffering or deprivation we endure here on earth, the greater our reward in Heaven. Suffering was thought to be an important part of the earthly trials which would fit us for the life hereafter. The administration of chloroform in childbirth (which Queen Victoria helped to pioneer) was strongly

187

opposed by many leading clerics on the ground that the agony of childbirth was God's will. In our humanitarian age few of us can bear the idea that God wills intolerable pain, either as a punishment or as a purification. Hence the hospices which do such devoted work in relieving pain but believe that each patient should go in God's good time. If you accept that from birth to death you are in God's hands, and that your function in this life is to serve Him and do His will, the idea of self-destruction must be akin to blasphemy. It is abhorrent also (strangely, to me) to spiritualists. I once talked with the elderly twin daughters of that famous spiritualist Sir Oliver Lodge, who was the grandfather of a young neighbour of mine. Both twins were serenely convinced that they were in constant communication with their dead husbands. 'But if they are, so to speak, only just the other side of the curtain,' I asked, 'why don't you take steps to join them?' They were inexpressibly shocked. It was against God's will; it would, in some unspecified way, *prevent* the reunion they so desired.

The second main objection to euthanasia comes from the doctors. The comfortable escapist view of many people that 'the doctors will see to it' that we do not linger in agony cannot be warranted — even though many doctors doubtless do ease the way out — for a medical 'mercy killer' is undoubtedly at risk of prosecution for murder. In 1969 a 'representative body' of the British Medical Association affirmed the fundamental objective of the medical profession as 'the relief of suffering and the preservation of life' and strongly supported the British Medical Association's condemnation of euthanasia. In my experience, doctors tend to say, 'Dying patients seldom ask to die and rarely to be killed.' It is not uncommon, though, for people dying in misery to plead with son, daughter, husband or wife to put them out of their misery, as they would sadly but calmly, put to sleep an old and suffering dog or cat. Probably the knowledge that doctors take a big risk in administering a lethal dose inhibits patients from asking them for release. But I think many people feel, as I do, that no one has a right to put the onus for ending his or her life on to another person, and perhaps especially not on to a doctor, whose whole training and life's work have put the emphasis on life *saving*. If we believe that every human being has the 'right to die', which is the claim of EXIT, we should accept that it is a right to terminate *one's own* existence, not to put the burden on any other person, even the most devoted spouse, parent or child.

That means, of course, that one must acquire early enough the means of ending one's life with dignity and as painlessly and expeditiously as possible, which is why I welcomed the decision of the 1979 annual meeting of the Voluntary Euthanasia Society (as it then was) to prepare and publish a booklet, for members only, which in the course of discussing suicide would include details of how to make *sure* of ending one's life and not bungling the attempt. As Arthur Koestler said at the meeting which took this decision, 'There is only one nightmare worse than intolerable illness, and that is bungled suicide.' I was grateful to one of the reporters at this meeting, Corinna Adam of the *Guardian*, for making it clear that the members present were not cranks or melancholics. 'Once the decision to choose when one has had enough is taken, people seem to become splendidly cheerful. A more robust, determined group of old people you would have to go far to find . . . They were like idyllic advertisements for what old age should be like. It is their determination to last like that for as long as possible and then go out quickly and neatly that puts the sparkle in their eyes' (And the jokes in their mouths, I would add. At this very meeting I had a conversation with a man from Somerset, who said that he had become acquainted with a botanist who had helped him to identify hemlock. 'I make wine,' he said with a twinkle. 'I don't see why I shouldn't distil myself a potion of hemlock.') Two months later it was reported that the membership of the society had doubled, from 2,000 to 4,000, and within a year rose to 10,000.

Most of the rather over-heated discussion in the media of the decision to publish a 'suicide booklet' centred on the third main objection to euthanasia — that old people would be pressurized into ending their lives by unscrupulous relatives. It is possible that this might happen, just as it is possible that the booklet might get into the hands of a youngster depressed about his/her A-Levels or a collapsed love affair. There could be cases of relatives putting pressure on the unwanted old to make an end; there could be cases of young people dying who ought not to die. But such cases will be very, very few, and we should never forget that there will always be those who will choose to die before their time, whatever safeguards we institute. North Sea gas does not kill; it is because of that, not the existence of Telephone Samaritans, it is said, that the suicide rate has fallen. But suicides still occur. Seriously depressed young people do not necessarily resort to drug overdoses. Alas, they slash their wrists, they jump out of high windows or off high bridges into the Thames or the Avon at Bristol — and such suicide bids are almost invariably fatal, whereas swift medical treatment can save the lives of the pill-takers. (The pill-takers, in fact, are often uttering a cry for help rather than planning a certain termination. Their subconscious will to live is likely to make them underestimate rather than overestimate the fatal dose.)

As for the unwanted old whose covetous or mean-spirited relations are supposed to be so eager to despatch them, I should have thought that they would be very unwilling to cling to life without love and by no means unwilling to accept a means of getting off the hook. Better to die quickly by one's own will than to linger, neglected, despised, resented and disliked. That way one could at least keep one's dignity. That is how *I* feel − but then it is a good many years since I took it for granted that it is necessarily better to be alive than dead. There are many more people who feel, as Archbishop Murphy does, that the existence of a legal 'right to die' and knowledge of how to exercise that right would put pressure on many old people to commit suicide because of the fear of becoming a burden on their families. Few families, indeed, do wish to get rid of the burden of looking after old parents, and most would be deeply grieved and shocked by such a suicide, which always must seem to imply that they had failed in love and care. I sympathise with this argument. But I still think that every human being has as much right to die as to live, and that if we have a mind to go in our own time, we have to weigh up this desire against the responsibilities we should be shedding and the hurt we should be causing.

The truth is that most normal young people have a very strong will to live − naturally and rightly, for this is nature's way of ensuring the survival of the race. Therefore many of them cannot understand why anyone should wish to cut the cord. They are apt to reject as 'morbid' any discussion of dying and death. Older people who have coped with serious adversity tend to reject euthanasia as the 'coward's way out'. Is it so cowardly? It must take immense courage to battle on against pain as, for instance, arthritic sufferers do, day by day, month by month, year after year. But that irrevocable step, the leap over the edge of the cliff into utter darkness, into the unknown and unknowable, must take great courage too, especially as, in our society, that deliberate step must be taken alone. I have often thought that in a humanist society, as ours has largely become, the ideal end of life would be a kind of Socratic farewell — a gathering of all one's treasured friends, and then, while the glow of their affection is shining brightly, the cup of hemlock or its modern equivalent, the willing and tearless farewell. It is our custom to celebrate the departure of our most admired friends with a memorial service. We must all have said to one another on these occasions, 'If only X could be here. Do you think he possibly could be, in spirit? He would have enjoyed it so much.' Will there ever come a day when X could be present at a *pre*-death ceremony and gather round himself the cloak of his friend's love and esteem before going through the door into the unknown?

A letter in the *Guardian* gave a moving account of how the writer's mother had taken a large overdose after six operations for breast cancer and brain tumour at the age of fifty-four. She arranged every detail so that her husband and family should be caused the least possible distress. 'She always had a thing about suicides leaving a mess for others to clear up. She was still writing an explanatory note when she died.' For me the most heartening part of this courageous and kind woman's story is that her daughter could write, eight years later, 'In no way can I or would I want to regret having had a mother who committed suicide in this way. The unselfishness of the act continues to be a source of admiration.'

It is often said that death is as much a taboo subject in Elizabeth II's Britain as sex was in Victoria's. I doubt if this is so in the last quarter of the twentieth century. People do talk about dying and about death. There are many discussions in serious newspapers and on television and radio. But what we seem unable to discuss, except occasionally in highly abstract and speculative terms, is whether there is any existence after death, and if there is, whether it can be a personal survival or a merging into some impersonal life force. I doubt if many older people would admit nowadays to being afraid of death, though they may well be afraid of dying because of the fear of pain or the loss of faculties. My friend, the old people's chaplain, said, 'I find the vast majority of people have an anxiety about death because of its uncertainty.' And the churches, he suggests, are partly to blame for this, because 'we have not used the material at hand for festivals such as All Saints and All Souls and the Communion of the Saints.'

Hasn't the Church stopped telling us what to expect? The collects of the Anglican Church are full of references to the life everlasting and prayers that we may 'after this life have the fruition of thy glorious Godhead', or 'pass to our joyful resurrection', or 'fail not finally to attain thy heavenly promises'. Sunday by Sunday Anglicans declare their belief in the 'resurrection of the body'. The service for the burial of the dead prays for 'our perfect consummation and bliss in

193

body and soul, in thy eternal and everlasting glory'. Symbolic language, of course. But symbolic of what? It is taken for granted nowadays that we have lost our fear of hell. That old story of the minister who fulminated against the child who laughed in the kirk: 'Ye will not laugh in hell, boy', those murals found in very old churches which show fiends prodding sinful souls into the everlasting fires with pitchforks, strike us with horror. There does linger in some people, though, a fear of retribution for wrongdoing, or at least an unease as to what purgatory or purification may await them. People who feel this unease indulge sometimes the fantasy that reincarnation would give them a chance to improve on their performance in this life and to work their way upwards, through various incarnations, to a respect-worthy life style and personality which would earn its reward in 'heaven'. But I have not been able to find any such consoling image in those Hindu scriptures that I have seen. This passage from the *Markandeya Purana* is far from reassuring: 'A man repeatedly goes through a cycle of births and deaths. In this way he is like a clock on the wheel of the world. Sometimes a man attains heaven, sometimes he goes to hell, and sometimes a dead man repeats both heaven and hell. And sometimes, born again in this earth, he reaps the fruits of his own acts. And sometimes, enjoying the fruits of his own acts, within a short time he breathes his last.'

So having lost the fear of hell and having never acquired belief in reincarnation, we have, most of us, lost also the hope of heaven, in the sense that our forefathers so fervently held it, as a 'better place', somewhere 'up there'. Heaven as a 'place' tends to be something of a joke, a picture of a fierce old St Peter questioning applicants and admitting the successful ones to an eternal life, of listening to angels harping and belting out a Handelian *moto perpetuo*. It is true that occasionally one may still see in the 'In Memoriam' columns of local newspapers this touching little verse:

> The last trump sounded,
> The angel said 'Come',
> The pearly gates opened,
> And in walked Mum.

But the sorrowing relations do not really visualize Mum shaking hands with St Peter or learning to play the harp. They don't, rightly, visualize anything at all, and I think it sad that the Church and the humanists give them so little help. Would not *any* kind of compelling imagery help to take the sting out of death of our loved friends and deny the grave its victory? As J.B. Priestley put it, 'Isn't it time to give heaven a chance?'

The Victorians had these certainties, and the minor novels of the age are full of deathbed scenes which show total confidence in the 'better life' ahead. In Mrs Henry Wood's *Johnny Ludlow* a pointsman named Lease says on his deathbed: 'The great dark load seems to have been lifted off me and light to be breaking. Don't sob, Polly. Perhaps father will be able to see you from up there as well as if he stayed here.' And Mrs Wood's Jake the Gypsy breathed, 'Carrie has gone up to be an angel in heaven. She's waiting for me. It was for the best she should go. God has been very good to me. Instead of letting me fret after her or murmur at lying helpless, He only gives me peace.'

I personally have met very few Christians who believe in reunion with those who, in the old-fashioned phrase, have 'passed on'. One widowed friend said to

195

me, 'I do know I hold firmly to some kind of continuing life. Whether we shall "meet again" I don't know, and I don't think I mind. Yet the idea of the Communion of Saints is very precious. If I came to believe that this present life was all, and then out with the candle, I shouldn't want to go on living at all. It would indeed be "a tale by an idiot, signifying nothing".'

I talked about these things with the Rev Paul Oestreicher, vicar of the Church of Ascension, Blackheath, and well known for his work with Amnesty International. He said very firmly that the concept 'this is Earth and there is Heaven' he regarded as 'a cosmology that even for old people is no longer really credible'. So how does he deal with ideas of death and the hereafter in his parochial work?

> I believe it is important to show that in our Christian faith we have already, here and now, entered what I call 'eternal life'. I see it as my main task to take hold of whatever faith a dying person has. If there is some measure of belief that God is in charge within this life and beyond it, not many words are needed. Holding a person's hand, literally and metaphorically, one hopes to take him across a barrier that is a great psychological hurdle — and for some also a great physiological burden associated with pain and the fear of pain — and to assure him that the actual process of death is totally painless and is a kind of gliding out of the body, as we have known it here, into whatever a loving God has in store for us.

But Paul Oestreicher will not even attempt to give people any kind of verbal or visual image of the hereafter in terms of *place*, only in terms of conditions. He reassures his flock:

You will be in a no less trusting and no less loved relationship with a God who cares and who will take you on the next phase of your pilgrimage. I can hold your hand up to the threshold, but at that point Someone Else is going to take your hand and guide you into an area that will probably be a progression from what we are now to what we are called to be. What that is, or what shape it may take, I haven't a clue, and I don't think I want to know. I don't want to create false images. There is no place out there called 'heaven'. There is a totally new quality of life in a totally incomprehensible context that none of our spatial terminology is relevant to.

Many agnostics like me are able to respond to that kind of thought. Yet the confidence those Victorians had that they would meet their beloved parents, husbands, wives, children, friends is enviable. Such a waste, I have often thought, if I can never communicate in any form whatsoever with those most dearly loved people who enriched my life for too short a time. Paul Oestreicher said:

As we are created personalities, as there is a distinctive ME, I do believe that I am not going to merge into infinity. The created personality has some ultimate meaning, and if that meaning is in relation to a Creator who also loves us and others are also in that relation, then in some mystical sense that I can't define, I think my relationship with those I love cannot only be sustained on death but deepened and matured by it. I think this is not only possible but probable.

It is not only committed Christians and spiritualists of course, who are convinced of personal survival. In his remarkable book *Over the Long High Wall* J.B. Priestley wrote: 'Death as a falling asleep for ever, as a giant never-failing sleeping pill with everything over and done with at last, seems to me a fairly soft option . . . Such reasoning power as I possess compels me to reject this idea of death. I just can't make it fit into the patterns I must accept. It can't claim to be a scientific verdict any longer.' Priestley talks a language I can relate to. I have said myself that in nature nothing is wasted, for when the plant dies it makes humus in the soil for other plants to use, and that though matter may change its nature, it does not cease to exist. What is more, the brain has electrical charges that cannot be 'seen' but can be recorded. When the television set is switched off, the electro-magnetic waves it picks up do not cease to flow. Is there an analogy here with the brain?

Priestley puts it pungently.

Certainly it can easily be proved that at death the body's time is up. But that is all that can be proved and we are entitled to ask for more than that. To say that we have had our answer is to say that the visible world is everything and the invisible world nothing, and this is to be behavioural to the point of insanity. Consciousness can survive the death of body and brain because while they inform it and strongly influence it, they don't own it.

In his later book *Instead of the Trees* he points out that no one says 'I AM a body.' It is always, 'I HAVE a body.'

Priestley believes that part of the self or psyche is

able to escape from the limitations, temporal and spatial, to which body and brain are strictly subject. 'It does not have to obey the time and space regulations of science to the annoyance of less open-minded scientists still shouting "All nonsense and coincidence".' His bitterest attacks are on 'Dr Knowall' who defies anyone to prove that there is life after death — 'but why should he not be pressed into producing proof that death ends all?'

Many elderly people must share my feeling that it would help if we had a firmer framework for our thinking about what *form* survival might take. We cannot know, of course. It is interesting that the accounts of people who technically have 'died' through illness or accident but have returned to life almost all tell of a sensation of great light and warmth. Wally Cameron, a Toronto musician, was quoted in the *Observer* Colour Magazine as saying that he felt himself to be up on the ceiling of the operating theatre looking down at his physical body, 'like an old used car that I didn't want any more'. There was a great white light, which he followed through a tunnel. 'It was all around me, but the major part of it was in front of me, moving. And in front of the light was a very relaxed, overwhelming feeling of release.' The light led this man to a door which he opened — and on the other side was his father, who had died two years before.

A Canadian director of human resources, who had clinically 'died' more than thirty times, had a number of 'after-life' experiences, all of which were similar, in that he felt 'a bright, radiant light and the sensation of warmth coming around me. I vividly recall the feeling of being approached by a bright light, an extremely brilliant radiance.' It is interesting that Tolstoy, in

199

one of his most powerful stories, *The Death of Ivan Ilyich* — about a man who spent many months in physical torment before he accepted that the whole of his life's assumptions had been wrong — described in Ilyich's last hours this same sensation of a beckoning light. 'He searched for his former habitual fear of death and did not find it. "Where is it? What death?" There was no fear because there was not death, either.

In place of death there was light.

"So that's it," he suddenly exclaimed aloud. "What joy!"

Dr Mervyn Stockwood, recently retired Bishop of Southwark, who has been interested in psychical research almost as long as he has been an Anglican priest, put into words better than anyone I have met the impossibility of conveying what life hereafter may be like.

> If a baby in the womb were capable of conversation with a person outside the womb, it might say, 'Now tell me, what is life like in the world?' How could you say, 'Well, there is a war going on in Afghanistan?' Or, 'They are launching a rocket,' or that you had fish and chips for lunch? These concerns would be meaningless to the baby because he could only discuss — if he could discuss at all — in terms which were known to him. How can a butterfly communicate with a caterpillar? The conditions under which a butterfly lives are totally different from those under which a caterpillar lives and presumably are incomprehensible.

So, says Dr Stockwood, he is not at all surprised when people say that such communications as are alleged to come 'from the other side' are virtually meaningless. 'A person on the other side can only describe what it is like there in terms of this world. Many of the communications I have witnessed at seances seem to me banal. But how could it be otherwise?' (Dr Stockwood thinks that the fact that people resort to seances in their first moments of grief is natural and understandable, but that once they have had the reassurance that communication is possible with those whom they have loved, there isn't very much point in going on with it.)

It may be helpful to churchgoers of all denominations to indicate Dr Stockwood's *Christian* reasons for survival, for he believes that if there is no life after death, the whole Christian Gospel is in vain. 'In the prayer book,' he says, 'there are three creeds: the Apostle's Creed, where they say, "I believe in the resurrection of the body" the Nicene Creed, where they say they believe in "the life of the world to come"; and the old baptismal creed, which specifies "the resurrection of the flesh".' All rather difficult concepts for the agnostic to cope with, but Dr Stockwood says:

We take the Nicene Creed's statement about "the life of the world to come" as saying that when death comes to us it is not the end, but the gateway to something else, a fuller life, another dimension. The Apostle's Creed is more explicit, saying not only that there is some sort of existence after this one, but also that just as in this world our personalities have to express themselves through a body, so when we go on to another dimension our personality will have a 'body' of some sort. I shall remain as I am; you will remain as you. The third statement is rather more difficult. It does not mean that the actual flesh will be resurrected but that life in the next world will be associated with our life in this world, with our own present bodies. I have no difficulty in accepting the spiritualists' concept of the etheric body. I think it is very much what the New Testament means by the 'spiritual body' — that we have a sort of duplicate body which extricates itself at the time of death.

The Creeds can all be made more meaningful, thinks Dr Stockwood, by reference to St John looking into the tomb and, by seeing it empty, reassuring himself that Jesus is alive; by Mary Magdalene meeting the 'gardener' and being assured by His voice that He is the Risen Jesus; and by Doubting Thomas's being convinced by being allowed to 'reach his finger' into the nail marks on Jesus's hands and feet and the marks of the spear in His side. 'This is how I understand the three statements of the Easter story in the Creeds — the life of the world to come, the resurrection of the body and the resurrection of the flesh.'

But Dr Stockwood is insistent that you can't *prove* that someone still lives.

You can't *prove* that a person loves another person. He may have gone and rescued her from drowning because her husband or father is the boss of the concern and this act of bravery would get him promotion. You can't prove things of the spirit. You can only say 'It would appear so'; and when I have sat with people and had psychic communication from my friends and my family it would seem that they are the people they say they are. But to what extent these things may be coming out of my own mind, or from some complex system of thinking and of memory patterns, I don't know. I have had some convincing experience . . . but at the same sitting you may have communications which make no sense at all.

Like most of us, Dr Stockwood doesn't believe in reincarnation (perhaps a little regretfully?) but he asks:

What on earth is the point of Creation unless we can do something useful? If you believe there is a creative purpose at all, there must be some Mind, somewhere. This great world couldn't have come into existence out of nothing. Whoever did this, the originator was not going to these enormous pains for us for just a piddling seventy years of life. We must believe that there is some purpose, somewhere, for mankind.

Do we believe vaguely in some sort of survival, or do we believe in a meaningful life after death? Dr Stockwood says with urgent conviction:

I have no desire just to survive, to continue seeing people of whom one may have had too much already. That's a thought that fills me with dismay. But to continue a life of useful service and heightened opportunities, that is something which is enormously exciting. Go back to the analogy of the caterpillar. Just to nibble cabbage leaves isn't very exciting, but compare that with the enormously exciting existence of the butterfly.

Are we all, then, assured of a tranquil passage, at the end, into a new and perhaps more gloriously purposeful existence? Dr Stockwood is cautionary.

The current thinking is that God is a decent chap and will fit us all in. I think what is missing today is the note of judgement. Ought we not to prepare ourselves for what lies ahead? If you are called to prepare for a sports team, and six months before the critical day you are guzzling and drinking and that sort of thing instead of going into training, you may not make the team. In this way we should try to prepare ourselves for the fuller life, instead of arriving maimed, with our whole attitude distorted by egocentricity, which is the curse of life in this world.

So whether our concept of dying is that it is fearful or hideous, or is just a slipping of the bonds that tie us to life in this world, is perhaps largely a matter of our temperament and the philosophy or system of beliefs we have adopted. *I* have never thought that we should be frightened of the actual moment of death since a small spaniel who had been tormented with fits for the last day or two or her short life settled down on my lap and gave up the struggle with a gentle little sigh. Will it be, as Mervyn Stockwood suggests, a reversion to the 'nappy stage' in which we came into this life? 'You arrive in this world helpless and usually you leave it helpless.' Will it be surrounded by sorrowing family, as so often pictured in Victorian deathbed scenes? Or alone and frightened in the dark? Too quickly to know what is happening? In hospital with the curtains ominously drawn round the bed? (In the Sue Ryder Foundation hospice at Leeds they leave the curtains open, so that patients can feel the comradeship of other patients right to the end.) Or shall we, as in Dylan Thomas's poem, go down fighting?

Do not go gentle into that good night,
Old age should burn and rage at close of day;
Rage, rage against the dying of the light.

Or shall we have certainty, as in Thomas's other fine, fierce poem: 'And death shall have no dominion'?

Can we believe, perhaps, with Maude Royden, one of the first English women to be ordained, that 'beauty is our proof that God is love', and that 'the atheist and the agnostic can sit down with the Christian before great beauty, whether natural or of art, and find that this beauty brings peace to the soul'? — and that the awe with which one sees or hears the greatest works of man, like the roof of the Sistine Chapel or Bach's B Minor Mass, suggests that human consciousness is not finite but is part of the infinite, a universal immanence? No 'message' has come through to us from Shakespeare, or Dante, or Bach, or Goethe, or any of the great communicators of past centuries — but how could it, as Mervyn Stockwood says, in any form we could comprehend?

There are many people who, in middle life, find great comfort in their belief that one day their life will come to a full stop. As Priestley put it, 'They have had enough of life, with all its aches and pains, worry and fuss, strain and stress and will be glad when it is all blotted out, once and for all.' Or if life, despite frustrations or tragedies, still provides a richly rewarding experience, one can still think of it as a drama which somehow would be deprived of meaning if it were not completed by a final curtain. I think that was rather my own view in earlier years, and I have never felt any confidence in everlasting life or any great yearning for it.

But in my later years I have thought sometimes

that death might be a doorway. To what? Something, perhaps, like the 'awareness' that Willa Cather described in the words of the narrator, Jim Burdon, of her novel *My Antonia*:

I was something that lay under the sun and felt it, like the pumpkins, and I did not want to be anything more. I was entirely happy. Perhaps we feel like that when we die and become part of something entire, whether it is sun and air or goodness and knowledge. At any rate, that is happiness, to be dissolved into something complete and great. When it comes to one, it comes as naturally as sleep.

Sources of Further Information

Books

Ronald Blythe, *The View in Winter* (Allen Lane, 1979)

Ivor Brown, *Old and Young* (Bodley Head, 1971)

Willa Cather, *My Antonia* (Virago, 1980)

Alex Comfort, *A Good Age* (Mitchell Beazley, 1977)

Doris and David Donas, *Young Till We Die* (Hodder & Stoughton, 1973)

Irene Gore, *Age and Vitality* (Unwin Paperbacks, 1979)

Help the Aged, *A Handbook for Retirement: The Time of Your Life* (1979)

Robert Kastenbaum, *Growing Old* (Harper & Row, 1980)

Fred Kemp and Bernard Buttle, *Looking Ahead: A Guide to Retirement* (Continua Productions, 1977)

David Loshak, *Daily Telegraph Guide to Retirement* (Collins, 1978)

Harry Miller, *Countdown to Retirement* (Hutchinson Benham, 1978)

Kate Millett, *Sita* (Virago, 1977)

Chris Oram, *Going Well Over 60* (World's Work and *Sunday Times,* 1979)

J.B. Priestley, *Instead of the Trees* (Heinemann, 1977)

J.B. Priestley, *Over the Long High Wall* (Heinemann, 1972)

Peter Townsend, *The Last Refuge* (Routledge & Kegan Paul, 1962)

Virginia Woolf, *Diaries* (Hogarth Press, 1977—8)

Periodicals

Choice, monthly magazine published for the Pre-Retirement Association, Bedford Chambers, Covent Garden, London WC2E 8HA

New Age, quarterly magazine of Age Concern, Bernard Sunley House, 60 Pitcairn Rd, Mitcham, Surrey CR4 3LL

Old Age, annual register of social research published by the Centre for Policy on Ageing, Nuffield Lodge, Regent's Park, London NW1 4RS

YOURS, monthly newspaper for the elderly, available from PO Box 126, Watford WD1 2HG

Organizations

Age Concern, Bernard Sunley House, 60 Pitcairn Rd, Mitcham, Surrey CR4 3LL

British Association of Retired Persons, 14 Frederick St, Edinburgh EH2 2HB

British Pensioners and Trade Union Action Committee, c/o Islington Task Force, 10 Corsica St, London N5

Buretire, Health Centre, Market Square, Bishop's Stortford, Herts

Centre for Policy on Ageing (formerly the National Corporation for the Care of Old People), Nuffield Lodge, Regent's Park, London NW1 4RS

CRUSE (National Organization for Widows and their Children), 126 Sheen Rd, Richmond, Surrey, TW9 1UR

Employment Fellowship, Drayton House, Gordon St, London WC1H 0BE

EXIT: Society for the Right to Die with Dignity (formerly the Voluntary Euthanasia Society), 13 Prince of Wales Terrace, London W8 5PG

Galleon World Travel Association, Galleon House, King St, Maidstone, Kent ME14 1EG

Help the Aged, 32 Dover St, London W1A 2AP

Holiday Fellowship, 142—4 Great North Way, London NW4 1EG

Link Opportunity, Bernard Sunley House, 60 Pitcairn Rd, Mitcham, Surrey CR4 3LL

National Association of Widows, c/o Stafford District Voluntary Service Centre, Chell Rd, Stafford ST16 2QA

National Benevolent Fund for the Aged, 12 Liverpool St, London WC2

National Council for the Single Woman and Her Dependents, 29 Chilworth Mews, London W2 3RG

National Federation of Housing Societies, 30—53 Southampton St, London WC2 7HE

Over Forty Association for Women Workers, Mary George House, 120—122 Cromwell Rd, London SW7 4HA

Pensioners' Voice (National Federation of Old Age Pensioners' Associations), 91 Preston New Rd, Blackburn, Lancs BB2 6BD

Pensions Campaign Centre, Transport and General Workers Union, 16 Swains Lane, London N6

Pre-Retirement Association, 19 Undine St, London SW17 8PP

Public Appointments Unit, Civil Service Department, Whitehall, London SW1

REACH (Retired Executives Action Clearing House), 1st Floor, Victoria House, Southampton Row, London WC1B 4DH

Right to Fuel Campaign, 7 Exton St, London SE1 8UE

Saga (Senior Citizens) Holidays Ltd, 119 Sandgate Rd, Folkestone, Kent CT20 2BN

Success After Sixty, 14 Great Castle St, London W1N 8JU

Index

211

214